L E X I P R O

A N G L A I S

Les mots-clés du tourisme et de l'hôtellerie

4ᵉ édition

Joëlle Rouanet-Laplace
Enseignante à la Faculté de Sciences économiques
de Montpellier

Bréal

1, rue de Rome 93561 Rosny cedex

© BRÉAL 2008
Toute reproduction même partielle interdite
ISBN : 978 2 7495 0464 3

Avant-propos

Ce lexique s'adresse aux étudiants et aux professionnels du secteur tertiaire.

Il s'adresse à tous ceux qui désirent acquérir ou perfectionner les notions fondamentales propres à l'anglais du tourisme.

Il convient tout particulièrement aux étudiants préparant l'épreuve d'anglais des BTS Animation et gestion touristiques locales, Ventes et productions touristiques et Hôtellerie-Restauration.

Cet ouvrage est conçu comme un outil de travail et s'efforce de cerner les principaux problèmes afférents au tourisme et d'offrir au lecteur un panorama aussi complet que possible de la langue touristique.

Le vocabulaire sélectionné est présenté à partir du français, puis mis en contexte grâce à des exemples notamment extraits d'articles de *BBC News, The Economist, The International Herald Tribune, The Guardian, The Independant* afin de permettre une meilleure assimilation et d'éviter tout contresens sur l'emploi de tel ou tel concept.

Ce lexique est complété par 2 index, l'un de toutes les entrées françaises, l'autre de toutes les entrées anglaises.

Cette quatrième édition a été entièrement revue et augmentée afin de tenir compte des dernières évolutions du secteur du tourisme.

L'auteur.

Sommaire

ALPINISME ET SKI
Mountaineering and skiing

alpinisme
mountaineering
The high season for all mountaineering in the western Alps is from the beginning of July to mid-September.
Often compared to the Himalayas and Andes, the Tetons present serious and daunting mountaineering challenges during the winter.

alpiniste
mountaineer / climber
Coolidge was an American-born British historian and mountaineer who, in the course of about 1,750 ascents, made one of the first systematic explorations of the Swiss, French, and Italian Alps.
The resort town of Chamonix lies at the foot of the Mont Blanc, which is popular with both skiers and climbers.

alpin
alpine
This picturesque alpine resort, nestled in the valley, offers a variety of well-serviced runs.

altitude
elevation
Yosemite Valley enjoys mild winters because of its 4000-foot elevation.

à 2 000 m d'altitude
2000 meters above sea level / 2000 meters above the level of the sea

altipiste / altiport
snow runway / mountain landing strip

après-ski
after-ski / après-ski
After-ski in Zermatt is very lively.
Several restaurants cater to the hungry skier and bars provide pleasant after-ski entertainment.

ascension
ascent
Sherpas are essential to the ascents of various mountains of the Himalayas.

ascencion en solitaire
solo ascent
He made the first solo ascent of Mount Mac Kinley.

faire l'ascencion de
to ascend (a mountain) / to climb (a mountain) / to make the ascent of
Two Scottish climbers died after falling 1,500ft onto rocks while climbing a mountain in the French Alps.
Whymper, an English mountaineer, was associated with the exploration of the Alps and was the first man to climb the Matterhorn.

avalanche
avalanche / snowslide
Thanks to their training and experience guides have the ability to assess a slope for avalanche risk or pick a safe route through a glacier's hidden crevasses.

appareil de recherche des victimes d'avalanche (ARVA)
avalanche transceiver / avalanche beacon / avalanche bleeper
By using transceivers buried skiers and boarders can be found quickly.

couloir d'avalanche
avalanche gully
The access track to Manganui Ski Area crosses "The Manganui Monster" avalanche gully. It is not uncommon most seasons to have avalanche debris within the gully area. Visitors and the public are advised not to loiter in the avalanche gully.

déclencher une avalanche
to trigger an avalanche / to spark an avalanche
A handful of skiers who have triggered avalanches have been prosecuted for acting irresponsibly and endangering lives.
The Alps are known for the local "Föhn" effect – a warm wind that blows on the Southern side of mountain slopes, raising the temperature by several degrees and often sparking avalanches.

être emporté par une avalanche
to get caught in an avalanche / to be hit by
an avalanche
Getting caught in an avalanche must be a terri-
fying experience.
The group was hit by an avalanche in the Gran
Paradiso National Park near the French
border.

risque d'avalanche
avalanche hazard
Even if the avalanche hazard is low, always
carry a transceiver, a shovel and a probe.

zone d'avalanche
avalanche area

barrage
dam
The dam is under construction.

bâton de marche
walking pole

bâton de marche télescopique
telescoping walking pole / collapsible
walking pole

bâton de ski
ski pole / ski stick

bois
woods

boisé
wooded
A densely-wooded valley.

bosses
moguls

brèche
notch

canons à neige
snow cannons

cascade / chutes d'eau
cascade / water falls / falls
Nine hundred miles northwest of Buenos Aires, in
the steamy tropical rain forests of Missione, the
thundering falls of Iguazu form one of South
America's greatest natural spectacles.

chaines (véhicule)
chains / snow-chains
The snow blocked dozens of roads and several
mountain passes; some were subsequently closed
or left only accessible by the use of snow chains.

chasse neige
snowplough

col
pass / saddle
This pass is often impassable in winter.

cordée
rope

premier de cordée
first on the rope

être encordé
to be roped together
The climbers were roped together across the
mountainside so if one slipped the other could
halt their fall.

s'encorder
to rope up

corde
rope
Ropes are used for abseiling.

crampons
crampons
He was learning to ice climb using crampons
when several tonnes of ice fell and buried him.

crête
ridge

crevasse
crevasse

culminer
to soar / to tower
Much of the island is mountainous; the highest
point, Mount Misery, soars some 3,792 feet into
the tropical sky.

damer
to groom
This resort offers 40 miles of groomed cross-
country ski trails.

dameuse / machine à damer
snow-grooming machine

descendre une piste
to go down a slope / to plummet down
a slope / to ski down a slope
Take a helicopter ride to some remote spot to ex-
perience the exhilaration of skiing down virgin
slopes.

descente à skis
ski descent
Mrs Murray was the first female Scot to climb Mount Everest and the first person to complete a telemark ski descent from the summit of the coldest mountain in the world, Alaska's Mount McKinley.

descendeur
downhill skier / downhiller

descendre en rappel
to abseil

descente en rappel
abseiling
There are lots of opportunities for skiing, rock and ice climbing, abseiling and mountain biking in the Cairngorms.
No previous abseiling experience is required for this expedition.

descendre des rapides
to raft / to run rapids / to run a river

descente des rapides
rafting / rapids running / river running
This trip was one of the best water experiences: five days of action-packed rafting through unspoilt rainforest wilderness.

descente en eau vive
white water rafting
Try our whitewater rafting expedition that gets deep into the Australian wilderness.
Outdoor activities include white water rafting, canyoning and gorge walking, archery and mountain biking.

domaine skiable
ski area / ski field
This resort covers a large ski area.
Rising from 1600 m to 2075 m, Mount Hutt ranks as one of the highest ski fields in the Southern hemisphere. The area has been nicknamed "the ski field in the sky".

donner l'alerte
to raise the alarm
Two members of the climbing group braved worsening conditions to raise the alarm at a remote mountain hut.

enneigement
snow conditions
Courchevel has a good history of snow conditions, but to cope with warm winters, it has a two-mile artificially created snow area.

Snow conditions at the top of Whistler and Blackcomb mountains are usually excellent – they see an average of 900 cm of snow a year!

équipement de ski
ski gear / ski equipment

s'équiper
to gear up
Let's gear up for the slopes.

être bien équipé
to be properly equipped
Mountain rescuers warned ramblers and climbers to be properly equipped before venturing into the Highlands.

équitation
horse riding / horseback riding

monter à cheval
to ride a horse / to go horse riding

promenade à cheval
horseback ride

piste cavalière
bridle path / bridle road / bridleway

escalader
to climb / to scale
Climb up to that top! You'll have a breathtaking view of the valley.
She scaled Everest by the arduous north face shortly and returned safely back down the most dangerous part of the mountain.

escalade / varappe
rock-climbing / climbing
With easy access and peaks that rise six to seven thousand feet off the Jackson Hole valley floor, the Tetons are one of the premiere climbing destination in the world.

mur d'escalade
climbing wall

s'étendre
to stretch
The Pyrenees are stretching from the Atlantic Ocean to the Mediterranean Sea dividing France from Spain.

fixation (ski)
binding
By using special bindings and skins, the ski tourer is free to roam the mountains at will.

fixation avant
toe binding

fixation arrière
heel binding

forêt
forest
Sherwood Forest, the home of legendary outlaw Robin Hood is under threat.

couvert de forêts
forested
The mountains are forested up to a certain altitude, giving way to alpine meadows before bare rock is reached at the highest points.

forfait
ski-pass / lift-pass
A five-day ski pass is included in the overall price. I have lost my lift-pass.

funiculaire
funicular / funicular railway
A funicular railway taking skiers to the slopes on Kitzsteinhorn mountain near Salzburg caught fire as it passed through the tunnel.

garde forestier
park ranger / ranger
The Dartmoor rangers are the eyes and ears of the national park authority, monitoring erosion, clearing up litter, assisting emergency services and working with the public to maintain the beauty of Dartmoor.

glacier
glacier
Glaciers are shrinking all over the planet.
If rising temperatures and low precipitation continue, many smaller glaciers will vanish in a decade.

glaciaire
glacial
Glacial lake / glacial valley

glisse
sliding
Novel ways of sliding have offered a challenge to those jaded by skiing.
Monoskis, ski-scooters and hang-gliders all enjoyed a boom.

guide de montagne
mountain guide
Local guides know where to find excellent safe snow conditions surprisingly close to the beaten track.

prendre un guide de montagne
to hire a mountain guide
Always hire a fully qualified mountain guide when skiing way off-piste or in glacial terrain.

hameau
hamlet
A secluded hamlet.

harnais
harness
For abseiling you will be kitted out with a harness and a helmet then attached firstly to a safety rope and then to a static abseil rope.

héliport
heliport

être héliporté
to be airlifted
They were airlifted to the glaciers.
A tourist suffering from hypothermia, stranded for three nights on New Zealand's highest mountain has been airlifted to safety.

imperméable (adj)
waterproof
Waterproof clothing and walking shoes are essential.

vêtements imperméables
waterproof clothing / waterproof clothes / waterproofs

jumelles
binoculars

lac
lake
The lake can be reached by a 500 mm gauge train which brings tourists along a precipitous track of about 6 miles with spectacular views.
Many beautiful glacial lakes dot the high country of Yosemite.

luge
luge / sled / sledge / toboggan

faire de la luge
to sled / to sledge / to toboggan
The children were tobogganing down the hill.

moniteur de ski
ski instructor
Qualified instructors will help you to perfect your technique and gain maximum pleasure.

cours de ski
ski lessons / ski instruction

école de ski
ski school

montagne
mountain
The Pyrenees are a range of mountains that separate France from Spain.
A visit to Georgia's mountains puts you knee-deep in beautiful scenery, pioneer history and genuine hospitality.

montagnes couronnées de neige
snow-capped mountains / snow-tipped mountains

chaine de montagne
mountain range / mountain chain / range of mountains / chain of mountains
The Andes are the second highest mountain chain in the world.
The San Gabriel and San Bernardino mountain ranges rise abruptly to peak over 10,000 feet, separating Los Angeles from desert lands to the north and forming an imposing backdrop for the teeming city.

montagneux
mountainous

mont
mount

motoneige
snowmobile

neige
snow / "white stuff"

neige poudreuse
powder snow / ungroomed snow / "cold smoke" (US)
Skiers manoeuvre over a series of moguls that make skis shatter in spite of the deep cushion of powder snow.

« soupe »
slush

neiges éternelles
everlasting snow

névé
ice-field / snow field

niché
nestled

Spend a skiing holiday in Zermatt, one of the all-time great resorts, nestled below the Matterhorn.

parapente (sport)
paragliding
Long known as an outdoorsman's paradise, Jackson Hole has evolved into a mecca for paragliding. Come and have the experience of a lifetime with a tandem flight from the top of Rendezvous Mountain.

paroi rocheuse
cliff / wall

paroi de glace
ice-cliff

patinage sur glace
ice skating / skating on ice
Skating on ice used to be a rapid form of transportation across frozen lakes, rivers nad canals.

patiner
to skate

patins
skates

patineur
skater

patinoire
ice rink / skating rink
The opening of the outdoor ice rink has been delayed.
Skate on an outdoor ice rink with spectacular views of Half-Dome and Glacier Point.

pente
slope
They had climbed the steep rock part and then had to traverse snow and ice on a slope.

pente douce
gentle slope

pente abrupte
steep slope

pic
peak / spitz
Mount cook is one of 22 peaks in the Aoraki and Mount Cook national park, attracting thousands of climbers every year.

à pic (vu d'en bas)
steep

à pic (vu d'en haut)
sheer

un à-pic
bluff / sheer drop

piolet
ice axe
Climbers use ice axes and crampons on rock as well as on ice.

pistes de ski alpin
ski slopes / runs
While many prefer to lounge on the beach for their main annual holiday, increasing numbers of people are turning their attention to the ski slopes for fun-packed winter holidays.
Every winter, millions of people flock to the slopes that were once the exclusive domain of the rich.

pistes de ski de fond
ski trails / ski tracks

pistes de ski artificielles
artificial ski slopes / dry ski slopes
Chatham dry ski slopes.
Plans for a £2m dry-ski slope centre in Cornwall have been revealed.

rafting
rafting / whitewater rafting
A whitewater rafting holiday in Peru.

randonnée (activité)
rambling / hiking
Rambling is the most popular activity in the Lake District.

faire de la randonnée
to ramble / to hike / to go rambling / to go hiking / to trek / to roam
What is it like to hike the Inca Trail?
The "right to roam" granted by the Country-side Act, allows walkers, runners and climbers to roam the access areas. Vehicles are not allowed.

une randonnée
hike / ramble / trek / walk
A trek which begins in Cumbria has been named among the world's best walks ahead of world-famous hikes to the Inca Trail, Everest and Mont Blanc.
The Coast-to-Coast walk takes in three national parks – the Lake District, Yorkshire Dales and North York Moors – and takes an average of 13 days to complete.

randonneur
rambler / hiker / roamer

Hundreds of ramblers took advantage of "the right to roam" as large areas of Northern England were opened up.
The "right to roam" excludes access to cultivated farmland and gardens, and roamers must obey local restrictions.

randonnée équestre
horse trekking
Horse trekking in Ireland.

randonnnée VTT
mountain biking
Teton Village, at the base of Jackson Hole Mountain Resort, is an excellent location for mountain biking. A seven mile network of single track trails has been created to increase the many dual-track trails already on the mountain. Beginner, intermediate, and expert rides can be found.

chemin de randonnée
trail / country lane
Bear Valley is the gateway to more than 100 miles of trails, providing access to the park's remote beauty for ramblers or horseback drivers.
The authorities in Peru have decided to limit the number of hikers to the popular tourist site, the Inca Trail. The trail ends at the ancient fortress of Machu Picchu.

guide de randonnée
hiking guide / walking guide

chaussures de marche
walking shoes / walking boots

raquettes (activité)
snowshoeing
Snowshoeing is gaining significant popularity among winter sports enthusiasts. It is a fantastic way to get out and about in the wintertime.
Snowshoeing offers the winter outdoor enthusiast the freedom of the summer hiker, and allows you a free rein to explore both on and off the beaten track.

faire une balade en raquettes
to go snowshoeing

raquettes
snowshoes
After sleeping in a Torino mountain lodge just over the border in Italy, they used snowshoes to reach the base of the craggy Tour Ronde.
Join a park ranger on a walk into the woods on snowshoes.

refuge
mountain hut / hut
To stay overnight at a mountain hut.
Tenth Mountain manages a system of backcountry huts in the Colorado Rocky Mountains connected by 350 miles of suggested routes.
The Alfred A. Braun Huts and Friends Hut are located in areas of known avalanche terrain with recurring avalanche cycles. Routes are not marked or maintained.

rive
bank (river) / shore (lake)

rivière
river

rocher
rock

sac de couchage / duvet
sleeping bag / down sleeping bag

sac à dos
rucksack / backpack

saison de ski
ski season
Winter sports bring millions of tourists and dollars to the Alps every year, and many resorts now rely on the ski season for 70 % to 80 % of their income.

secourir
to rescue
Specially trained guides patrol glaciers rescuing injured or exhausted skiers.

secouristes / sauveteurs / équipe de secouristes
rescuers / rescue team
Trained doctors could become part of mountain rescue teams, or be taken along on organised treks or climbs.
The helicopter evacuation of the climbers and their six rescuers was delayed by snow and strong winds but eventually went ahead.

ski
skiing
The Olympic Winter Games present five disciplines of skiing: alpine, cross country, ski jumping, Nordic combined, freestyle and snowboarding.
Most resorts are starting to diversify in the hope of attracting tourists who have other interests than skiing.

ski alpin
alpine skiing / downhill skiing

ski d'été / ski sur glacier
summer skiing / glacial skiing
Summer skiing is becoming more popular with skiers not just heading for the glaciers in Europe but branching out to the ski areas of Argentina, New Zealand, Australia and Chile.

ski de fond
cross-country skiing
If you have never tried cross-country skiing, tuition is available at most ski schools.

ski hors piste
off-piste skiing
Many skiers yearn to venture off-piste and feel the thrill of carving their signature in fresh powder snow.

ski de randonnée
ski mountaineering / ski touring / touring
Touring combines the technical pleasures of alpine skiing with the freedom of cross-country skiing.

héli ski
heliskiing
Heliskiing is off trail, downhill skiing that is accessed by a helicopter.

monoski
monoskiing

télémark
telemark skiing

skier / faire du ski
to ski / to take to the slopes

skieur
skier
Courchevel boasts miles of runs to suit everyone, from the dedicated advanced skier right down to the beginner.

skieur débutant
beginner

skieur intermédiaire
Intermediate skier

skieur confirmé
advanced skier

skieur chevronné
expert skier

skis
skis

location de skis
ski hire
Ski hire is easy. Book all your gear before you go.

snowboard / surf des neiges (sport)
snowboarding
Many resorts still offer only skiing and snowboarding. That's a big trap they need to get out of.

planche de snowboard / snowboard
snowboard
Snowboards come in several different styles, depending on the type of riding intended.

parc de snowboard
snowboard park
There is also a snowboard park with a half-pipe as well as a tubing park, which provides hours of fun for all ages.

sommet
peak / summit / mountain top
Sir Edmund Hillary of New Zealand was the first person to set foot on the summit of Mount Everest, the world's highest peak.
Touching the Void is the story of two British mountain climbers who stared death in the face while climbing a treacherous peak in the Peruvian Andes.

vaincre / atteindre un sommet
to conquer a summit / to reach a summit / to make it to the top (fam.)
Mountaineering means discovering new peaks to conquer.
A Londonderry dentist has become the first Northern Ireland woman to conquer Mount Everest.
They failed to reach the summit due to exhaustion and atrocious weather conditions.

sports d'hiver
winter sports / snow sports
Most of Nevada winter sports areas cluster around Lake Tahoe.
Snow sports carry a high degree of risk. There are plenty of ways to reduce the danger starting with training and equipment.

spéléologie
potholing / spelunking
Spelunking is exploring caves left in their natural state, wiggling along on hands and knees through narrow passages and tight spaces.

station de ski / station de sports d'hiver
ski resort / skiing resort / winter resort
Badger Pass – California's oldest ski resort – offers great downhill skiing.
Some of Switzerland's most famous ski resorts have published a report looking at the consequences of global warming on their winter tourist business. Winter resorts under 1,500 metres should not focus on skiing as their main attraction.

station de montagne
mountain resort
In the wake of Europe's heat wave in 2003, mountain resorts saw an increase in tourists who had decided that a beach in Greece or Spain would be simply too hot.

station village
traditional resort (≠ purpose-built resort)

survie
survival

couverture de survie
survival blanket / space blanket
A rucksack is essential for carrying a shovel, food, a first aid kit and a space blanket.

kit de survie
survival kit

téléphérique
cable-car / gondola
The fastest cable-car in the world can carry 1900 skiers an hour up to a 1700 metre run.
Five people were injured after a cable-car derailed and crashed to the ground.

télésiège
chairlift
An early snowfall attracted enthusiasts to the resort over the weekend but they were left on the ground when the chairlift remained closed.

téléski / remonte-pente / tire-fesses
ski lift / T-bar / ski tow
Ski lifts whisk skiers to heights otherwise accessible only by a day's climb.
One of this resort's greatest asset is a mind-blowing complex of ski lifts which have virtually eliminated the need to queue.
Several ski tows will lift beginners to the easy runs.

torrent
torrent / stream / mountain stream

Mountain lakes and streams offer good catches all year, making the Shasta region an angler's paradise.

traineau
sled / sledge / sleigh
Visitors can board a horse-drawn sleigh for a ride through woods of spruce and fir past moose dipping their heads into a mountain stream.

promenade en traineau
sled ride / sledge ride / sleigh ride
Why not go for a sledge ride behind husky dogs?

vallée
valley / vale / dale
The Owens valley lies between California's two highest mountain ranges: the Sierra Nevada and White Mountains.
A huge part of Russia's valley of the Geysers, considered as one of the greatest natural wonders in the world.

vélo tout terrain (VTT)
mountain bike (MTB) / all terrain bicycle (ATB)

vêtements de ski
ski wear / ski clothing
New materials such as carbon fibre and titanium have improved ski equipment, while new fibre and insulating materials have improved ski clothing, offering skiers increased comfort and freedom.
High performance and high style ski wear is all the rage!

blouson de ski
ski jacket

bonnet de ski
ski hat

cagoule / passe-montagne
balaclava / balaclava helmet

casque
helmet

chaussures de ski
ski boots

combinaison de ski
ski suit

gants de ski
ski gloves

lunettes de ski
goggles

pantalon de ski
ski pants

tenue de ski
snowsuit

veste polaire
fleece jacket

volcan
volcano
Lying underneath Yellowstone Park it is one of the largest volcanoes in the world.
The California cascade range includes two gigantic glaciated volcanoes: the dormant 14162-foot Mount Shasta and the still active 10457-foot Mount Lassen.

en activité
active
The volcano became active again last year after being dormant for centuries.
Chile is one of the most volcanic countries on earth, with more than 100 active volcanoes.

éteint
dormant / extinct
The eruption of the Chaiten volcano caught local authorities by surprise, as experts say it has been dormant for more than 9,000 years.

volcanique
volcanic
Emergency plans have been put into operations after two new craters opened on the summit of the volcanic island of Stromboli.
All remaining inhabitants of the island of Stromboli have been evacuated amid fears of further violent volcanic eruptions.

CLIMAT / TEMPS / SAISONS
Climate / weather / seasons

anticyclone
anticyclone
Anticyclones generally bring fair weather and clear skies.

anticyclone des Açores
The Azores anticyclone / The Azores High.

arc-en-ciel
rainbow
"Rainbow to windward, foul fall the day. Rainbow to leeward, rain runs away."

atmosphère
atmosphere

atmosphérique
atmospheric
Atmospheric conditions / atmospheric pressure.

aube
dawn
"The rosy-fingered dawn."

à l'aube
at dawn

augmenter
to rise / to increase

hausse des températures
a rise in temperature / an increase in temperature
There's been a steady rise in temperature after some relief due to heavy rain.

aurore australe
aurora australis / southern polar lights

aurore boréale
aurora borealis / northern polar lights

baromètre
barometer
Whatever the season, you consult the barometer to see what the weather is going to be like.

pression barométrique
barometric pressure

briller
to shine (sun) / to twinkle (stars)
He was staring at the stars twinkling in the sky.

brise
breeze

brouillard
fog
Summer fog doesn't daunt the thousands of annual visitors who come to enjoy the charm and scenic beauty of Mendocino.

il y a du brouillard
it's foggy

bruine
drizzle
Drizzle is very fine rain, almost like mist.

bruiner
to drizzle

brume
haze (légère) / mist

se calmer (vent, tempête)
to abate / to subside
The storm eventually abated.
The ship will remain in port until the storm subsides.

calotte glaciaire
ice cap
The giant ice caps on Groenland and Antartica.

canicule
dog days / heat wave
The hottest times of the year are known as "dog days" in reference to the prominence of a star during that period.
Forecasts appear to rule out prospects of a sustained heat wave.

la chaleur
hot weather / heat

chaleur accablante / torride / suffo-cante
stifling heat / scorching heat / oppressive heat

chaud
warm

très chaud
hot

chuter (températures)
to dip / to drop / to fall
If you must cross Death Valley in summer, make sure your car is in good condition and travel at night when temperatures drop.

chute des températures
a drop in temperature / a fall in temperature

climat
climate
Southern California's main asset is its dry, subtropical climate.
The contrast of clear sunny days with a cold climate never fails to invigorate.

climat continental
continental climate

climat désertique
desert climate

climat méditerranéen
mediterranean climate

climat humide
moist climate

climat océanique
oceanic climate / maritime climate
Maritime climates are fairly humid, accompanied by high amounts of precipitation.

climat polaire
polar climate

climat tempéré
temperate climate

climat tropical
tropical climate
Much of the equatorial belt within the tropical climate zone experiences hot and humid weather.

climatique
climatic
Climatic conditions.

changement climatique
climatic change

domaine climatique / zone climatique
climate belt / climate zone
A number of climate belts can be traced between the equator and the pole in each hemisphere.
The tropical or equatorial zone is centred roughly on the equator.

courant (n)
current
The Gulf Stream is a warm surface current which originates in the Gulf of Mexico and flows across the Atlantic. It influences the climate of the UK and northwest Europe.

courants océaniques
ocean currents
Ocean currents such as the Gulf Stream are responsible for moving excess heat gained in the tropics to the poles, thus maintaining the Earth's thermal equilibrium.

couvert (ciel)
overcast
The grey overcast sky.

crépuscule
dusk / twilight

au crépuscule
at dusk / at twilight

cyclone
cyclone
Tropical cyclones are amongst the most powerful and destructive meteorological systems on earth.
Cyclone Sidr hit Bangladesh last year.

degré
degree

degré Celsius / degré Farenheit
degree Celsius / degree Farenheit
The temperature reached 38°Celsius yesterday. Last winter temperatures reached minus 36.4° Fahrenheit.

doux (climat, températures)
mild
Coastal temperatures are generally mild year-round.

éclaircie
bright interval / sunny spell / sunny period

Breezy conditions prevented an air frost at low levels and most places saw sunny periods during the day.

s'éclaircir
to clear up
It has cleared up now! Let's go for a walk!

équateur
equator
Three of the most significant imaginary lines running across the surface of the earth are the equator, the Tropic of Cancer, and the Tropic of Capricorn.

fonte des glaciers
melting of glaciers

frais
cool / fresh
Pine forests, hidden lakes and cool air lure vacationers year-round to the San Bernardino range.

rafraîchissant
cooling

se rafraîchir
to cool off
Sacramento sizzles in summer but residents and visitors cool off in the many lakes, rivers and mountain retreats nearby.

le froid
cold weather / cold
Heavy snowfalls, high winds and cold cause problems across northern Europe, causing major disruptions to transport and power supplies.

une vague de froid
a cold snap
A cold snap is a short period of cold and icy weather.

froid
cold / chilly
The hot days of summer fade into warm autumnal months tempered by chilly mornings and evenings.

être transi de froid
to be chilled to the bone / to be numb with cold

fuseau horaire
time zone
What time is it in every time zone?

glace
ice

gel
frost
With relatively clear skies and lighter winds, a frost is likely overnight.

gelée blanche
hoar frost

geler
to freeze
Brooks, rivers and lakes are frozen to the delight of kids always fond of skating.

il gèle à pierre fendre
it's freezing hard / it's freezing solid

givre
glazed frost / ground frost

girouette
weathercock / weather wane / wind wane

grêle
hail
One of the most notorious places for hail is the area in the USA from Texas to Montana, and from the foothills of the Rockies to the Mississippi River, known as "Hail Alley".

grêler
to hail

grêlon
hailstone
It is in the tropics, where the largest clouds develop, that the largest hailstones form, which are often the size of golf balls.
The largest recorded hailstone measured 46.7cm in circumference.

hémisphère
hemisphere
The equator divides the planet into the northern and southern hemispheres.

hémisphère nord
northern hemisphere
During the northern hemisphere summer, the North Pole receives 24 hours daylight while the South Pole experiences 24 hours darkness.

hémisphère sud
southern hemisphere

héliographe
sunshine recorder

heure d'été
daylight saving time (DST) / summer time

Beginning in 2007, most of the United States begins Daylight Saving Time at 2:00 a.m. on the second Sunday in March and reverts to standard time on the first Sunday in November.
In the European Union, Summer Time begins and ends at 1:00 a.m. Universal Time (Greenwich Mean Time). It begins the last Sunday in March and ends the last Sunday in October.

humide
humid / moist / wet / damp
Persistent rain left the roads wet and slippery.

humidité
moisture / dampness / humidity

inondation
flood / flooding
The widespread devastation caused by cyclone Sidr and by monsoon floods damaged the winter harvest.

inondé
flooded
Most English Channel ferry crossings were cancelled, and dozens of roads were flooded or closed, including the M25.

latitude
latitude
Latitude provides the location of a place north or south of the equator.

longitude
longitude
Zero degree longitude is located at Greenwich, England.

se lever
to arise (wind) / to lift (fog)
The fog finally lifted around 11 a.m.

lune
moon
Astronomers gathered to watch the moon slip into darkness.
Total eclipse of the moon.
The moon is in its third quarter.

clair de lune
moonlight
Moonlight produces mirage effects and weird landscapes.

méridien
meridian

The vertical longitude lines are also known as meridians. They converge at the poles and are widest at the equator.

Méridien de Greenwich
Prime Meridian / International Meridian / Greenwich Meridian

météo / temps
weather
The weather is very changeable.
California's biggest asset might be its weather: lots of sun, little rain and low humidity make it possible to enjoy outdoor activities all year round.

quel temps fait-il ?
what's the weather like?

le temps est au beau fixe / variable / mauvais
the weather is set fair / changeable / bad
As anyone who lives in the UK knows, the weather is highly changeable at times!

un temps de saison
seasonal weather

une période de mauvais temps
a spell of bad weather
Parts of the United States are preparing themselves for a spell of bad weather as experts predict that some of the strongest winds of the season are due.

être bloqué par les mauvaises conditions météorologiques
to be weather bound

bulletin météorologique
weather report

bulletin d'alerte météo
weather warning
The weather warning carries the possibility of localised flooding as well as trees and other debris being blown onto the roads and increased side winds.

émettre un bulletin d'alerte météo
to issue a weather warning / to issue a warning.
As the national meteorological service for the United Kingdom, the Met Office has a vital role in public safety. The Met Office warns the community of severe or hazardous weather by issuing a warning.
Severe weather warnings have been issued.

carte météorologique
weather chart

conditions météorologiques
weather conditions
Adverse weather conditions.

Office National de la Météo
The Met Office (UK)
Going abroad? Find out the latest weather conditions before you travel. The Met Office Weathercall Holidays is updated daily, and offers the latest five-day forecasts and climate reports for more than 200 holiday resorts and cities worldwide.

prévisions météorologiques
weather forecast / forecast
The BBC Weather Centre based in London's BBC Television Centre produces around a hundred forecasts every weekday, over 22 hours each week, as well as additional broadcasts over the weekend, for its national and international channels.
The news ended and the weather forecast began.

prévisions météorologiques à 5 jours
a five-day forecast

station météorologique
weather observation station / weather station

mousson
monsoon / monsoon rains
The strongest monsoons are those which affect India and southeast Asia.

neige
snow
Snow is expected on Friday at all resorts.
Snow has fallen at most resorts in America seeing a return to powder skiing in most states.

enneigement
snow conditions
What are the latest snow conditions?
The snow conditions are typically spring-like with packed pistes in the morning which soon soften under the heat of the sun.

bulletin d'enneigement
snow report

chute de neige
snowfall
Bumper snowfalls in Canada have left powder on the slopes at many resorts.
Heavy snowfalls over the weekend in the Alps have improved conditions for snow sports at most European resorts.

coulée de neige
snowslide

cristaux de neige
snow crystals

flocons de neige
snow flakes

neiger
to snow

neigeux
snowy
It has been a snowy weekend for the Austrian resorts and the conditions for the week ahead look promising.

nivomètre
snow gauge

nuage
cloud

nuageux
cloudy
Partly cloudy / cloudy with sunny spells.
Skies are cloudy and temperatures are in the mid to upper 30s.

orage
thunderstorm
A thunderstorm is brewing.

couver / se préparer (orage)
to brew

orageux
thundery

ouragan
hurricane
New Orleans was devastated when hurricane Katrina hit the Gulf Coast in August 2005.
The island is in the path of the hurricanes in the Caribbean.

pleuvoir / pleuvoir à verse
to rain / to pour

il pleut des cordes
It's raining cats and dogs.

pluie
rain
The morning rain gave way to sunny spells and scattered showers in the afternoon.

pluie verglaçante
freezing rain

averse
rain-shower / shower
A few showers developed across the north.
Thursday's predominant weather is forecast to
be heavy showers.

chute de pluie
downpour / rainfall
Rainfall totals will be above average in Wales,
Northern Ireland, western Scotland and most of
England.
The rainfall in desert areas is less than 250 mm
or 10 inches per year, and some years may
experience no rainfall at all.

le temps est à la pluie
it looks like rain

pluvieux
rainy
In July the rainy weather did not improve and
many parts of Scotland were flooded.

pluviomètre
rain gauge

Pôle nord / Pôle sud
North Pole / South Pole
Even today, reaching the North Pole is a difficult
and challenging journey.

étoile polaire
North Star / polar star / pole star / polaris
The North Star is nature's compass.
The polar star is the beacon of all travellers in
the northern Hemisphere.

nuit polaire
polar night
During the polar nights which last six months
at the poles, temperatures fall to extremely low
values.

précipitations
precipitation / drizzle / rain

rafale
squall / gust (wind) / flurry / blizzard
(snow)
The Met Office said that gusts of 60 to 70 mph
were expected with the possibility of 80 mph gusts
on exposed coasts and hills.

réchauffement
warming
The warming of the Atlantic is likely to create a
large number of hurricanes.

réchauffement de la planète
global warming

se réchauffer
to warm up / to heat up
Very wet summers as well as intense heat waves,
storms and droughts are coming thicker and
faster as the world heats up.

saison
season
The four seasons: spring, summer, autumn, winter.

automne
autumn / fall (US)

été indien
Indian summer
The American Meteorological Society's Glos-
sary of Weather and Climate defines Indian
summer as "a time interval, in mid – or late au-
tumn, of unseasonably warm weather, generally
with clear skies, sunny but hazy days, and cool
nights".

saison sèche
dry season

saison humide
wet season

saison des pluies
rainy season

soleil
sun

au lever du soleil
at sunrise

au coucher du soleil
at sunset

soleil de plomb
scorching sun

ensoleillé
sunny
Sunny weather is forecast this week-end.

ensoleillement
sunshine
The Met Office figures have revealed record
sunshine and below average rainfall.

gorgé de soleil / noyé de soleil
sun-drenched / sun-soaked
Hawaii's palm-fringed beaches are constantly
sun-soaked and ventilated by light tradewinds.

souffler
to blow

For much of the year, Northeast tradewinds blow across Southeast Asia.

température
temperature

Death Valley has the dubious honour of having recorded America's highest temperature (134 °F in July 1913).

au-dessus des normales saisonnières
above the seasonal average / above average

Temperatures will stay well above the seasonal average in all parts of the British Isles.

au-dessous des normales saisonnières
below the seasonal average / below average

Temperatures will be well below average.

un écart de température
a range of temperature

tempête
storm / gale

There are warnings of gale in southeast Ireland. The Caravan Park was partially submerged after yesterday's storm breached defences and left mobile homes teetering on the edge of the sea.

tempête de neige
snowstorm / blizzard

tempête de sable
sandstorm

Tourists were stuck in a sandstorm.
A caravan of camel riders in a sandstorm.

être bloqué par une tempête
to be stormbound

The ferry was stormbound at Dover.

tremblement de terre / séisme
earthquake

A magnitude 5.6 earthquake struck in a rural area northeast of San Jose, California, Silicon Valley's biggest city, causing minor damage.
An earthquake of magnitude four is equivalent to 1,000 tonnes of TNT.

secousses
tremors

Tremors reached seven on the Richter Scale.

échelle de Richter
Richter Scale

tropique du Cancer
tropic of Cancer

The tropic of Cancer lies 23°27' north of the equator.

tropique du Capricorne
tropic of Capricorn

The tropic of Capricorn lies 23°27' south of the equator.

tsunami
tsunami

On December 26, 2004, a 9.0 magnitude earthquake struck off the Indonesian island of Sumatra, triggering a tsunami that killed tens of thousands of people in Indian Ocean coastal communities.

typhon
typhoon

A typhoon sank a sailing-boat in the Pacific Ocean, drowning 8 people.

vent
wind

The Mistral is probably the best-known wind in Europe.

alizés
trade winds / tradewinds

The Caribbean, located between the Equator and the tropic of Cancer, enjoy warm sunshine tempered by light tradewinds for the greater part of the year.

venteux
windy (weather) / windswept (region)

It's a very windy day today.
Chile is a land of contrasts occupying a long coastal strip from the arid Atacama Desert in the north to the wild and windswept region of Patagonia in the far south.

battu par les vents
battered by the winds

Britain is bracing itself for a second day of storms today as forecasters warned almost the entire country would be battered by gale-force winds tonight and into tomorrow.

verglacé / glacé
icy

The roads were treacherously icy.

HÉBERGEMENT
Accommodation

1

HÔTELS
Hotels

---

accueil
welcome

accueil personnalisé / accueil chaleureux
personalised welcome / warm welcome

accueillir
to welcome

animal domestique
pet
Pets are welcome.

catégories d'hotels
hotel types

classement tourisme
official grading / grading system
Our grading system takes into account a wide range of criteria from service quality and facilities to scenery and hotel setting.

hébergement
accommodation / lodging (US)
This hotel is ideal for guests looking for an elegant accommodation at a reasonable place right in the centre of London.
All lodging within the park on the South Rim of the Grand Canyon is provided by Grand Canyon National Park Lodges.

hébergement agréé
approved accommodation
An enormous choice of approved accommodation awaits the visitor to Ireland.

hébergement en demi-pension
half-board accommodation / Modified American Plan (MAP)

Half-board prices under the MAP include an additional three-course dinner with coffee or tea.

hébergement en pension complète
full-board accommodation / American Plan (AP)
Full board is compulsory in season.

capacité d'hebergement
accommodation capacity

hébergement autonome, indépendent
self-catering accommodation / self-catering
Self-catering provides families with the freedom to holiday at their own pace.
Self-catering holidays are catching on.
Small hotels have adapted their premises to provide self-catering units, meeting the need for flexibility in touring holidays.

hôtel
hotel
Conferences, wedding facilities, golf holiday are the speciality of this old-established hotel.

hôtel de charme
character hotel

hôtel classe touriste
tourist class hotel
The tourist class hotels we have carefully selected represent excellent value for money.

hôtel de luxe
de-luxe hotel / luxury hotel

hôtel quatre étoiles
four-star hotel (official rating: four stars)

hôtelier (n)
hotelier / hotel-keeper
Europe's hoteliers experienced a difficult year in 1990.

hôtelier (adj.)
hotel
hotel amenities / hotel capacity…

chaîne hôtelière
hotel chain
Most hotel chains cluster around airports or in main cities.

industrie hotelière
hotel industry

résidence hôtelière
aparthotel / serviced apartments
Increasingly, in recent years, the busy executive has turned to serviced apartments in preference to hotels.

zone hôtelière
hotel strip

tenir un hôtel
to manage a hotel / to run a hotel
This pleasant hotel is most efficiently run by a charming couple.
A family-run hotel.

chèque-cadeau
gift certificates
Gift certificates are truly practical easy-to-offer gifts.

A
CHAMBRES
Bedrooms, rooms

chambre
bedroom / room
The bedroooms are all interior designed in English country-house style with marble bathrooms.
All the rooms and en-suite facilities have been totally renovated and refurbished with great care.

chambre avec bains
room with private bath / room with bathroom en-suite

chambre climatisée
air-conditioned room

chambre communicante / chambre voisine
connecting room / adjoining room

chambre pour deux personnes
double room / double-bedded room / twin room / twin-bedded room (lits jumeaux)

chambre individuelle
single room
The hotel has recently been totally interior designed and refurbished to a very high specification and offers 42 rooms-singles, twins, doubles-each with en-suite bath.

chambre familiale
family bedroom

chambre avec vue
room with a view

vue mer
sea view

vue montagne
mountain view

avoir vue sur la mer
to be sea-facing
All rooms are sea-facing with a balcony.

suite / suite de luxe / petite suite
suite / luxury, penthouse suite / junior suite
Our luxury suites have woodburning fireplaces and private ocean-view decks.

bien-aménagé / bien-équipé
well-appointed / well-equipped / appointed (with) / equipped (with)
All the rooms are superbly appointed affording the ultimate comfort.
A well-equipped country hotel.
A country inn equipped with all modern amenities.

calme (adj.)
calm / peaceful / quiet / tranquil / serene
Paddington is a quiet residential area-its streets reflecting the prosperous Empire days.

confort / confortable
comfort / comfortable
Having every amenity and the last word in comfort, this manor house is the perfect place for a rest.

donner (sur)
to overlook / to command a view on, over
The meals are served in our spacious dining-room commanding a sweeping view over the lake.
This hotel overlooks the charming little town of Etretat and enjoys spectacular views over the famous cliffs and the coastline.

lit à baldaquin
four-poster bed

meubles
furniture (sg.: a piece of furniture)

meubles d'époque
period furniture
Spacious en suite bedrooms are decorated with period furniture.

meublé
furnished
The rooms are pleasantly furnished in antique style.

B

SERVICES ET AMÉNAGEMENT
Hotel services and facilities

---

aire de jeux pour enfants
children's playground / children's adventure playground

aménagements pour les handicapés
facilities for the disabled / facilities for the handicapped / wheel-chair access

ascenseur
elevator (US) / lift

coffre-fort dans la chambre
safe deposit box / private safe

change
currency exchange

garde d'enfants
baby-sitting service

internet haut débit
high-speed internet access

navette gratuite
courtesy coach / courtesy shuttle

parking
car-park / garage facilities / parking facilities
Two car-parks are within walking distance of the hotel.
Parking facilities are available to all guests.

piscine couverte / piscine à l'extérieur
indoor swimming pool / outdoor swimming pool, open-air swimming pool

salle de gym
fitness centre

salle de réunion
meeting room

service de blanchisserie
dry-cleaning and laundry

tennis
tennis court

téléphone direct
direct dial phone

C

FORMALITÉS
Hotel formalities

---

annulation / annuler
cancellation / to cancel
A two-day cancellation policy.
Cancellations have to be made before 6 p.m. on the arrival date.

> **frais d'annulation**
> cancellation fees

arrhes
deposit
A deposit of £150 or 20% of the total cost – whichever is the greater – must be enclosed with this form to secure your booking.

> **verser des arrhes**
> to make a deposit payment / to pay a deposit
> *Deposit payments should be made at least two months prior to departure date.*

bon d'échange / bon de paiement
voucher
If your booking is guaranteed by a voucher, you pay for the room in advance and present the voucher on arrival.

> **bon de paiement émis par une ligne aérienne (MCO)**
> Miscellaneous Order / Service Order

clé / clef
key

clé magnétique / clé électronique
hotel keycard / magnetic key / electronic key

A hotel keycard can be used to purchase goods and services at a resort complex such as Walt Disney World.

complet
fully booked / no vacancy / no vacancies

I'm afraid we're fully booked this week-end. Sorry, no vacancies!

descendre (dans un hôtel)
to check in

She checked in at the Chelsea Hotel.

disponibilité / disponible
availability / available

Availability is limited unlike our service!

selon disponibilité / en fonction des places disponibles
subject to availability

enregistrement
check-in / registration

enregistrer
to check in / to register

Guests must check in at the front desk.

fiche (à remplir)
registration card / registration form

Would you fill in this registration form?

A registration card is used to record the full name, nationality, home address and signature of each guest.

heure d'arrivée / heure de départ
check-in time / check-out time

groupes
parties / groups

un groupe de 10
a party of 10

There are reductions for pre-arranged parties of 10 or more.

libre (chambre)
vacancy / vacancies

libérer (une chambre)
to vacate (a room)

It is standard practice for hoteliers to require that guests vacate their rooms by noon.

numéro vert
freephone number / toll-free number

1-800 numbers are toll-free numbers in the USA. Dial toll-free 1-800-228-2028 to make a reservation.

quitter (un hôtel) (*régler sa note*)
to check out

He checked out of the hotel this morning.

départ de l'hôtel, remise des clés
check-out

Express check-out... Goodbye at the drop of a key... Another reflection of our legendary dedication to service!

réservation
booking / reservation

We have much pleasure in confirming your booking of two single rooms with baths.

Bookings are made on a Saturday to Saturday basis.

réservation en bloc
block-booking

réservation par internet
e-booking

réservation en ligne
online booking

réservation par téléphone / par telex
telephone-booking / telex-booking

centrale de réservation
central reservation office

tableau de réservations
reservation chart

effectuer une réservation / réserver
to make a booking / to make a reservation / to book / to reserve

I'd like to book a twin-bedded room from the 21st of september to the morning of the 26th.

garantir une réservation
to secure a reservation

tarif / prix de la chambre
room rate

The average room rate reaches $200.

taux d'occupation (d'un hôtel)
occupancy rate

Hoteliers try to increase the occupancy rate by offering holidaymakers rock-bottom prices in the low season.

afficher (un taux d'occupation de...)
to post an occupancy rate of...

Corsican hotels posted an occupancy rate of 80% last summer.

taxe de séjour
residence tax (US) / sejourn tax

2
AUTRES TYPES D'HÉBERGEMENT
Other types of accommodation
---

appartement
flat / apartment (US)

Your apartment will only be a few steps away from the finest shops, restaurants and neighbourhood conveniences.

meublé
furnished apartment, furnished flat / self-catering flat

We offer you a large selection of stylish furnished apartments in elegantly restored Victorian homes.

auberge
inn

Set on a hillside, overlooking the vineyards, this charming inn will enchant every visitor.

auberge de jeunesse
hostel / youth hostel / community hotel (cotel, US)

They travelled through Europe, always staying in youth hostels.

Hostels provide travellers of all ages an inexpensive, friendly atmosphere for spending the night.

« Café-Couette » / chambre d'hôte
"Bed and Breakfast"

Part of the charm of B&Bs is the chance they offer visitors to learn about the area from their host and other guests; it's a good way to exchange ideas on activities, restaurants and "must sees".

camping (activité)
camping

Camping is not permitted along roasides, parking lots or day-use only areas.

The US Virgin Islands offer superlative camping on the stunning white-sand beaches.

faire du camping
to go camping

terrain de camping
campsite / campground (US)

Campsites are usually serviced by a cafeteria, convenience stores and showers in separate buildings.

Death Valley National Monument operates 9 campgrounds throughout the monument.

camping-car
camper / motorhome / recreational vehicle (R.V.) / van

Buy a recreational vehicle and you'll enjoy the lifestyle of the semi-nomad.

Vans come equipped with sleeping quarters, stove and refrigerator.

camping sauvage
free camping / rough camping (ant.: supervised camping)

caution
security bond / security deposit

A refundable security deposit will be required; it will serve as a guarantee regarding any damages and cost of telephone calls.

chalet
chalet

Designed to take full advantage of the spectacular view over Lake Wakatipu, this comfortable chalet boasts a large stone fireplace.

château
castle / chateau (pl.: eaus / eaux)

The chateaux of the Loire Valley were built during the reign of Charles VIII, in a region of outstanding natural beauty.

Perched on a hilltop, this secluded castle commands breathtaking views over the valley.

châteaux privés recevant des hôtes
private chateaux with guestrooms

chaumière
thatched cottage

A cluster of grey thatched cottages set against a thickly wooded hillside makes this part of Buckland-in-the-Moor one of the most photographed corners of England.

cottage
cottage

Try our idyllic hideaway and unique vacation resort of de luxe cottages set on a private island in the Caribbean Sea.

demeure de caractère
mansion

Secluded in its own park, this mansion will make you revive and appreciate the special charm of the past.

draps, linge de lit
linen

Linen is not always provided in self-catering apartments.

échange d'appartement / de maison
flat swap / home exchange / house swap

House swapping is one of tourism's booming trends.

échanger son appartement / sa maison
to swap one's flat / one's home / to exchange one's flat / one's house

More and more holidaymakers are swapping their homes with other families to cut the cost of going abroad.

ferme
farm / farmhouse

This farmhouse provides an attractive base for visitors who value fresh flowers, informality and quiet domestic efficiency.

logis à la ferme / hébergement à la ferme
farmhouse accommodation / farm-based accomodation

Farm-based accommodation is popular among holidaymakers whose lifestyle orientation is towards healthy food and natural outdoor life.

vacances à la ferme
farm holidays

Farm holidays have enjoyed considerable success in recent years.

gîte
holiday cottage / cottage / gîte

A gîte is a French holiday home that is available for rent. Gîtes are usually fully-furnished and equipped for self-catering.

The owners of a holiday cottage which appeared in the BBC's version of Jane Austen's Sense and Sensibility *said they were bracing themselves for a busy year.*

le gîte et le couvert
board and lodging / room and board

héberger
to put up / to accommodate

Small farmers in Italy are making ends meet by putting up guests.

Airlines have established connections with hotels to accommodate their passengers.

hostellerie
country house hotel / hostelry (US)

Built of local pink granite and typifying the style of architecture found on the island of Jersey, the Little Grove is a country house hotel with traditional values and service.

lodge
lodge

Luxury safari lodges in South Africa.

louer
to hire / to rent

To rent holiday accommodation.

They rented a luxury serviced apartment with all of London in easy reach.

agence de location
rental agency

maison d'hôtes
guest house

manoir
manor house

Southern England has its share of stately homes, but its greatest architectural wealth lies in the manor houses.

motel
motel / motorlodge

In this family-owned motel, you can be assured of a friendly and personalized service.

multi-propriété
time-share / timeshare

Timeshare is a scheme whereby an apartment or villa is sold to several co-owners, each of whom purchases the right to use the accommodation for a given period of the year.

acheter en multi-propriété
to buy (a flat, a house…) on a time-sharing basis

pension (de famille)
guest house

pensionnaire / hôte payant
paying guest

ranch
ranch

No holiday captures the spirit of America so completely as a stay on a western ranch.

séjour dans un ranch
ranching / ranch holiday

For the very best of western adventures, try ranching!

relais
country inn / countryside inn

répertorier
to list

The National Association of Agritourism lists 1,5000 farms offering hospitality from the Alto Adige to Sicily, and it estimates that there are at least 5,000 others that go unlisted.

repertorié
listed (ant.: unlisted)

résidence secondaire
second home

Increasing disposable income has led to massive growth in second home ownership in countries like Spain, Greece and Italy.

roulotte
horse-drawn caravan

If you are looking for a fun, rustic, on the move, country holiday, think of meandering for a week in a horse-drawn caravan through the country lanes of County Wicklow, south of Dublin, Ireland.

situé
located / set / situated

This two-bedroom flat is conveniently located in the centre of the London West End.

villages de vacances
holiday villages / holiday centres / holiday parks / holiday estates

Lyme Bay holiday village can cater for up to 500 people a week. As well as bed spaces, the holiday park provides community facilities used by local people including a gym, swimming pool and a nursery.

The holiday village operator Center Parcs has 4 villages across the UK, each set in 400 acres of forest with lakes and streams.

TOURISME BALNÉAIRE
Seaside tourism

abrité
sheltered

Ventnor, sheltered from the north wind by the huge mass of Saint Boniface Down, is one of the warmest holiday resorts on the island.

abriter de
to shelter from

The high promontory that shelters San Diego Bay from the Pacific Ocean offers great harbour views.

The Elephant and Cardamom Hills have always sheltered the narrow coastal state of Kerala from the rest of India.

air marin
sea air

Breathing in sea air makes you healthy.

algues
seaweed

amarré
moored / berthed

Moored along the front of the harbour are the smaller fishing boats that bring their catches straight into the restaurants.

amarrer
to moor / to berth / to bring (a boat) to a berth

postes d'amarrage
berths / moorings

Aberystwyth's picturesque harbour has been dramatically remodelled to provide permanent berths for over 100 vessels.

Nearly 40 new moorings are being created in two of Jersey's marinas in a bid to improve facilities for local boat owners.

aménagement du littoral
coastal development / shore development

The World Wildlife Fund has investigated the effect coastal development is having on the environment.

ancre
anchor

jeter l'ancre
to drop anchor

Land access to the estate is customarily restricted, but the nearby coastline is open to boaters who can drop anchor, swim, fish and go snorkelling.

anse
cove

Boulder Beach lies in a small cove and is protected from the wind by giant granite boulders.

aquarium
aquarium

A killer whale that has been the star attraction at Canada's largest aquarium for more than 20 years was moved to a Sea World in America.

archipel
archipelago

A one-resort-per-island policy separates guests from locals and from other tourists, giving a sense of isolation that is one of The Maldives archipelago's main selling points.

atoll
atoll

Life on remote atolls continues to fascinate and inspire writers.

baie
bay

The bay of Fish Hoek is very popular with pensioners and families and its big beach and calm waters offer plenty of space for games, swimming, walking and exploring.

baignade
swimming

The coastline offers an incredible diversity from sweeping sandy beaches that are perfect for swimming and sunbathing, to stormy narrow shores with crashing waves.

Swimming has been banned.

baignade interdite
no swimming
Red "no swimming" flags were posted on the beach.

baigneurs
bathers
Bathers should be aware that Seatown is a steeply shelving beach.

maillot de bain
swimsuit / bathing suit

bain de soleil
sunbathing

prendre un bain de soleil
to sunbathe

chaise longue
deckchair

bains de mer
bathing / sea bathing
Brembridge is a quiet seaside village with good bathing and wide firm sands at low tide.

baleine
whale
Whale watching holidays are all the rage.

bateau à fond transparent
glass-bottom boat
Glass-bottom boats explore the colourful undersea marine life and vegetation of the island's legendary clear waters.

bateau de pêche
fishing boat

béton
concrete
The concrete coastline of Spain.

bord de mer
seaside

bordé de
fringed with / lined with

plage bordée de palmiers
palm-fringed beach / beach lined with palm-trees

brisants
breakers / surf

brise
breeze
A gentle sea breeze.

bronzer
to get a suntan

bronzage
suntan

crème à bronzer
suntan cream

cabine de plage
bathing hut

cabane de plage
beach hut
Southwold is an English resort town full of an old world charm. The town has 300 beach huts, which stretch along the shore like the brightly coloured beads of a necklace.

cabotage
coastal navigation

caboteur
coaster

camper / faire du camping
to camp / to go camping

terrain de camping
campground / campsite
Most of Death Valley campsites have scenic backdrops ranging from whispering sand dunes to sweeping mountain views.

feu de camp
camp-fire

cap
cape / point

le Cap de Bonne Espérance
Cape of Good Hope

Cap Lizard (Cornouailles)
Lizard Point (Cornwall)

casino
casino
A £3.5m casino at a seaside resort in Norfolk is due to be officially opened.

jouer (pour de l'argent)
to gamble

machine à sous / bandit manchot
slot machine / one-armed bandit

char à voile
sand yachting / land sailing / land yachting
The beach at St Anne's is a leading venue for sand yachting competitions.

chasse sous-marine
spearfishing

cocotier
coconut

cocoteraie
coconut grove
Beautiful coconut groves line this paradise island.

combinaison (sports nautiques)
wetsuit

coquillages
seashells / shells
Waterfront stores sell souvenirs ranging from seashells, jewelry and T-shirts to model ships.

huîtres
oysters

moules
mussels

corail
coral
Divers explore coral canyons, caves and ledges, viewing a variety of coral.

côte
coast
The Mediterranean coast / The Pacific coast / The Atlantic coast…
Big Sur is one of California's most spectacular stretches of coast.

la Côte d'Azur
The French Riviera

côtier
coastal
Fort Point – the brick and granite coastal fortification underneath the Golden Gate Bridge – is open daily for tours.

crabes
crabs

crevettes
shrimps / prawns

crique
creek

dauphin
dolphin
Cardigan Bay is one of the last remaining places in the UK where bottlenose dolphins live.

The presence of the dolphins is one of the main reasons why Cardigan Bay has been chosen as European Special Area of Conservation.

déchiqueté (côte)
rugged
Much of the island is uninhabited with a great deal of its rugged coastline only accessible by sea.

découpée (côte)
indented
Greece is a mountainous country with a very indented coastline and it includes numerous islands in the Aegean Sea, the Ionian Islands in the west, and the large island of Crete, which lies in the middle of the eastern Mediterranean.

détroit
strait

Le détroit de Gibraltar
The Strait of Gibraltar
Gibraltar is a beacon that signals the position of the Strait of Gibraltar, the narrow neck which separates Europe from Africa and provides the only link between the Atlantic Ocean and the Mediterranean Sea.

Le Pas de Calais
The Strait of Dover / The Dover Strait
The Dover Strait is considered to be one of the world's busiest international seaways, used by over 400 commercial ships daily.

digue
dyke / dike

dune
dune / sand dune
Around a quarter of a million people visit Ynyslas every year, drawn by the wide expanse of sand, the flower-rich dunes and the envigorating sea air.

ensoleillé
sunny
All the main villages lie on the island's sunny west coast.

coin très ensoleillé
suntrap

noyé de soleil
sun-baked / sun-drenched / sun-soaked

étendue (n)
stretch / expanse

The long stretches of sand and water from Santa Monica to Long Beach are dotted with fishing piers and marinas.

falaise
cliff

"The White Cliffs of Dover".
Along the North coast of Devon, promontories of grey rock alternate with sheer, tall cliffs and long stretches of sand.

front de mer
sea-front / ocean-front / waterfront

Papeete is delightfully provincial and designed for leisurely wandering along the sea-front.
San Francisco's waterfront is its chief drawing card. Attractions around Fisherman's Wharf and Pier 39 draw most visitors.
Water-taxis shuttle pedestrians around the bay, making stops at major waterfront hotels.

garde côte
coast guard

Coast guards are patrolling the shoreline.

glace
ice-cream

vendeur de glaces (ambulant)
ice-cream vendor

golfe
gulf

île
island

The United Kingdom consists of England, Scotland, Wales, and Northern Ireland. Situated off of the northwest coast of Europe, these islands extend between 50° and 60°N.
Corsica, Sardinia and Sicily are Mediterranean islands.

les îles Britanniques
the British Isles

les îles Anglo-normandes
the Channel Islands

les Baléares
the Balearic Islands

les îles Éoliennes
Aeolian islands

îles paradisiaques
paradise islands

iode
iodine

Invigorating iodine.

jetée
jetty

jetée promenade
pier

Brighton's West Pier was restored to its former glory with the help of more than £10m of National Lottery cash.

langouste
lobster

large / haute mer
open sea

au large de la côte
off the coast

littoral
coastline / shoreline

South Africa occupies the southern tip of Africa, its long coastline stretching more than 2,500 km from the desert border with Namibia on the Atlantic coast southwards around the tip of Africa and then north to the border with subtropical Mozambique on the Indian Ocean.

maître nageur-sauveteur
lifeguard

Beach lifeguards help to keep Cornwall's beaches safe during the busy summer season.
Lifeguards have reported a big increase in the number of stinging jellyfish off the area's coastline.

bateau de sauvetage
lifeboat

The lifeboat was sent but due to the tide and swells at the base of the cliffs it was unable to get close.

marée
tide

The lifeboat was launched after three young girls were cut off by the tide at St Michael's Mount, Cornwall.

à marée basse
at low tide

à marée haute
at high tide

raz-de-marée
tidal wave

le flux et le reflux
ebb and flow

se laisser surprendre par la marée
to be cut off by the tide / to be trapped by the tide
Two walkers had to be winched to safety by helicopter after being trapped by the tide on Whitby beach.

marin (n)
sailor

un peuple de marins
a seafaring nation

marin d'eau douce
landlubber

loup de mer
sea dog

méduse
jellyfish
Visitors to the coast at Tremadog Bay in north Wales have been warned about a swarm of jellyfish in the area.

mer
sea
The Channel / The Adriatic Sea / The Baltic Sea / The Irish Sea / The North Sea / The Mediterranean Sea…

quel est l'état de la mer ?
what's the sea like?

étale
smooth

agitée / houleuse
rough

démontée
raging

grosse
heavy

moutonneuse
choppy

en mer
at sea

mouette
seagull

naturisme
naturism / nudism

naturiste
naturist / nudist
Naturist beaches

océan
ocean
The Antarctic Ocean / The Arctic Ocean / The Atlantic Ocean / The Indian Ocean / The Pacific Ocean.

palmier
palm-tree
A sun-kissed island, replete with shady palm trees and a hammock swinging in the fragrant tropical breeze.

palmeraie
palm grove

parasol
umbrella

pédalo
pedallo

location de pédalos
pedallo hire
Oddicombe is a shingle beach with sailing, paddleboats, pedallo hire and beach huts.

péninsule
peninsula
Situated on the southern tip of the Sinai peninsula, Sharm-al-Sheikh boasts long stretches of natural beaches, clear water for diving and a dramatic landscape, with the Red Sea on one side and Mount Sinai on the other.

phare
lighthouse
The Longships lighthouse stands off Lands End. Around 300 years of maritime history has come to an end in south-west England after the region's last manned lighthouse became automated.

gardien de phare
lighthouse keeper

phoque
seal

colonie de phoques
seal colony
Along the Namibian and South African coast there are about 24 seal colonies.
Cape Cross is well-known for its colony of Cape Fur Seals.

otarie
sea lion

plage
beach
Strand has a long stretch of white, sandy beach ideal for long walks, fishing and surfing and wind surfing are very popular.

plage de galets
pebbly beach / shingle beach
The mile-long shingle beach at Seaton sweeps from high cliffs in the west to the mouth of the Axe in the east.

plage de sable fin
sandy beach
This four-mile stretch of windswept sandy beach is a dramatic place to hike-though unsafe for swimming.

plages du Débarquement
landing beaches
Utah Beach and Omaha Beach were the two American landing beaches during the Second World War.

plage privée
private beach

plongée sous-marine
scuba-diving

plongée libre
skin-diving / snorkeling

plongée sans bouteille / apnée
free-diving

faire de la plongée
to scuba dive

plongeur
diver / scuba-diver / snorkeler
Sharm-al-Sheikh has been described as a deep-sea paradise, with snorkelers and scuba-divers attracted by an abundance of corals, exotic marine plants and rare tropical fish.

plongeoir
diving-board

plonger (gén)
to dive

masque de plongée
diving mask

palmes
swimfins

tuba
snorkel

port
harbour
San Diego's beautiful harbour offers parks for strolling, piers and embankments for fishing, boat-launching facilities and lots of places to watch the ships go by.

port de pêche
fishing harbour

port de plaisance
marina / recreational boat harbour / yachting harbour
Elizabeth Marina is Jersey's newest marina. It offers 564 berths that are also available to non-residents.

poste de secours
first-aid hut / first-aid post

presqu'île
peninsula

promontoire
headland / promontory
"Strange, introverted and storm-twisted beauty" – so the poet Robinson Jeffers described Point Lobos, the promontory jutting into the Pacific south of Carmel.

quai
wharf

qualité de l'eau
water quality
More than 93 % of 520 beaches tested weekly by the Environment Agency had their water quality judged as excellent and only two beaches failed.

pavillon bleu
blue flag
Pets are not be allowed on Britain's blue flag winning sands from the beginning of May through to the end of September.
Cemlyn Bay is one example of a beach that has blue flag quality water, but does not have the facilities to qualify for blue flag status.

plages arborant le pavillon bleu
blue flag beaches

se voir décerner le pavillon bleu
to be awarded the blue flag
To be awarded the blue flag, a beach must meet the following criteria: it must be clean, waste disposal bins must be available, an adequate

number of lifeguards and / or life-saving equipment must be available, no industrial or sewage-related discharges may affect the beach area and information about bathing water quality must be displayed.

rade
roadstead

râtisser la plage (à la recherche de coquillages et autres trésors marins)
to beachcomb
Why not spend the morning beachcombing for shells, before chilling out at the little beach café?

récifs coraliens
coral reefs
From the South Pacific to the Caribbean, coral reefs-which are among the most delicate of marine ecosystems-are bearing the brunt of climate change and other human-driven activities like coastal development, deforestation and unrestricted tourism.
A rapid decline in the world's coral reefs could damage national economies that rely on underwater sea life for tourism revenue.

La Grande Barrière de Corail
The Great Barrier Reef
The Great Barrier Reef is a site of remarkable variety and beauty on the north-east coast of Australia. It contains the world's largest collection of coral reefs.

régate
regatta
Up to 30 vessels took part in the Funchal 500 Regatta from Falmouth to Madeira.

requin
shark
Holidaymakers have fled Italian beaches near Rimini after a great white shark attacked a fishing boat off the Adriatic coast.

rivage
shore / shoreline

rocheux
rocky
Rocky coasts offer great opportunities for wildlife watching.

sable
sand
Cancun features the postcard image of white-sand beaches with a clear blue ocean.

pelle
spade

seau
bucket

sables mouvants
quicksands
Morecambe Bay is notoriously dangerous, with fast rising tides and quicksands.

sirène de brume
foghorn

être situé
to lie / to be located / to be situated / to be set
Set in a bay beneath Europe's highest cliffs, Cassis was developed by the Romans as a fishing port and became a popular stop-off for pirates in the Middle Ages.

soleil
sun / sunshine

au lever du soleil
at sunrise

au coucher du soleil
at sunset

paresser au soleil / lézarder / se dorer au soleil
to bask in the sun / to laze in the sun / to soak up the sun
She enjoyed soaking up the sun sipping exotic cocktails.

sous-marin / sous l'eau (adj)
underwater
An ancient underwater city has been found off the coast of south-eastern India. Divers from India and England made the discovery based on the statements of local fishermen and the old Indian legend of the Seven Pagodas.

sports nautiques
watersports / aquatic sports
Watersports include sailing, scuba-diving, surfing, windsurfing, water-skiing, yachting…

planche à voile
windsurfing

ski nautique
water-skiing

station balnéaire
seaside resort / seaside town / coastal resort

The UK's seaside towns are well past their heyday and will never go back to the way they were, but some are making a comeback under a different guise.

surplomber
to overlook sth / to jut above / over sth

Perched on a hill overlooking the coast, this restaurant is a favourite watering hole for locals and tourists.

A volcanic mountain range jutting above the Atlantic off the coast of Morocco, Madeira is a tropical Eden.

vacances au bord de la mer
seaside holiday / bucket-and-spade holiday (fam)

The smell of fish and chips, the squawk of seagulls and the splash of bracing briney waves... Few childhood memories are as evocative as that of the British seaside holiday, which holds a unique place in the national psyche.

vague
wave

vierge (intact / pas défiguré)
unspoilt / pristine

The Seychelles – a group of 115 islands in the Indian Ocean, more than 1,000 miles off the east coast of Africa – are famous for their wildlife, coral reefs and white, sandy, pristine beaches.

village de pêcheurs
fishing village

Unspoilt by progress, the ancient fishing village of Polperro is a Conservation Village surrounded by an area of outstanding natural beauty situated in a sheltered cliff inlet.

voile
sailing

No previous sailing experience is required.

faire de la voile
to sail

voilier
sailing boat

dériveur
dinghy

THERMALISME /
TOURISME DE SANTÉ
Spa and health tourism

abordable / accessible
affordable

algues
algae / seaweed

algothérapie
algeotherapy
Algeotherapy is deeply relaxing, detoxifying, re-balancing and relieves aches and pains.

améliorer
to improve
Are you looking for a healthy way to lose weight to get better and improve your health?

amelioration
improvement

bain
bath

bain d'algues
algae bath / seaweed bath
The thalassotherapy centre offers traditional seaweed baths, seaweed body wraps, hydrotherapy, massage, marine based facials, beauty treatments and sun bed.

bain d'argile
clay bath
Try clay and mud baths for wellness and detoxification.

bain de boue
mud bath
In Calistoga, a spa-town situated at the foot of Mount Helena, thousands of tourists slither into mud baths and slide into mineral pools.

bain bouillonnant
bubble bath

bain de vapeur / bain turc
steambath
The treatment consists of spray showers, steambaths and massages.

bains (établissement)
baths

The Roman baths were a social centre; in addition to cleansing one's body, one could take exercise, relax or read.

se baigner / prendre un bain
to bathe / to take a bath
Be sure to eat a light snack prior to bathing. Located in the heart of Bath, Thermae Bath Spa is Britain's original spa – the only place in the UK where you can bathe in natural hot waters. Bathing in heated seawater and freshly harvested seaweed will ease away aches and pains. It is also ideal for skin ailments.

bonnet de bain
bathing cap / swim cap

maillot de bain
bathing suit / swim suit

peignoir de bain
bathrobe
We ask that guests crossing the lobby from the swimming pool wear cover-up garments like a bathrobe.

serviette de bain
bath towel / towel

baignoire
bath

balnéothérapie
balneotherapy / spa therapy
Since antiquity, balneotherapy has been used to relieve pain and stress.
Spa therapy is the act of bathing in thermal or mineral waters. It is most commonly prescribed for patients with psoriasis or rheumatoid arthritis.
Spa therapy is an effective treatment for chronic low back pain patients.

faire de la balnéothérapie
to undergo spa therapy
They underwent spa therapy in Vittel for three weeks.

bénéfique (à / pour)
beneficial (to)

This treatment can be beneficial, especially to young children.

bien-être
well-being / wellness
Tourism centred around the concept of health and wellness is a relatively new phenomenon in the UK market.
People from all around the world come to Calistoga for health and wellness.

bienfaits
benefits
The health benefits of water have long been established. A swimming pool not only offers the chance to improve cardiovascular fitness and muscle tone, but it also aids relaxation.

faire du bien
to do (someone) good
It will do you good.

boue
mud
Hungary's most renowned spa town is Heviz, set on the world's largest warm-water lake. Mud from the bottom of these waters is said to be particularly effective for rheumatism.

centre / établissement de remise en forme
health farm
Indulge and pamper yourself at a health farm.

contre-indications
contraindications
She had no contraindications to spa therapy.

être contre-indiqué
to be contraindicated

cosmétiques
cosmetics

cure
cure / thermal cure
A cure is not always a sinecure!
This extremely luxurious and futuristic spa offers all the facilities for a thermal cure.
Thermal cures stimulate recuperative powers and accelerate recovery.

cure d'amaigrissement
slimming course / weight-loss programme
Weight-loss programmes are administered under nutritional supervision.

commencer une cure d'amaigrissement
to kickstart a weight-loss programme / to embark on a weight-loss programme
Whether you are looking for a healthfarm break to kick start a weight loss programme or simply to pamper yourself with beauty treatments and relaxing massage you're sure to be impressed with our award-winning facilities.
They are going to embark on a weight-loss programme.

faire une cure / prendre les eaux
to take a cure (at a spa) / to take the waters
Cheltenham's spa waters gained in popularity in 1788 when George III spent five weeks "taking the waters" in the town to improve his health.
Taking the waters at resorts across Europe became fashionable for the rich.

curiste
cure-taker / spa-goer
Healthy, pure and natural, this environment offers cure-takers an ideal setting for a regenerative rest.
As visiting a spa becomes a more integral part of people's lifestyles, an increasing number of spa goers will combine the occasional luxury spa travel experience with regular visits to local spas.

curatif
curative / healing
Curative properties / healing virtues / healing waters…
Appreciation and understanding of the curative properties of natural mineral springs and seawater are less deeply ingrained in British culture than in many European, Asian and Arab societies.

détente
relaxation
They hope to generate a new income by treating visitors to a day of relaxation and beauty treatments.

se détendre
to relax
After a day of touring the wine country, you can swim in our warm mineral pool, relax on the sun deck, and rejuvenate with our famous spa treatments.

diététique (n)
dietetics

diététique (adj)
dietetic / diet
For decades, companies have made fortunes selling health and diet products to women.

dieteticien
dietician

diurétiques (n)
diuretics / water pills
Diuretics help to remove excess water from the body.

diurétique (adj)
diuretic
Diuretic qualities.

(se) dorloter
to pamper (oneself)
Why not tailor a short break to celebrate a special occasion or pamper yourself with a well deserved rest?
Spa and wellness holidays offer the opportunity to relax and pamper yourself.

douche
shower

douche à affusion
affusion shower

douche à jet
jet shower
The jet shower is effective in anti-cellulite treatments.

douleur
pain

douleurs rhumatismales
rheumatic pains

douloureux
painful / sore

eau minérale
mineral water
Deeside mineral water comes direct from nature, flowing from the historic Pannanich Wells near Balmoral Castle in the heart of the remote Scottish Highlands.

eau minérale gazeuse
sparkling mineral water
Perrier is the number one naturally sparkling mineral water in the world.

eau de source
spring water

enveloppement
body wrap
We feature soothing massages, luxurious herbal facials, and detoxifying body wraps.

enveloppement d'algues
seaweed wrap
Seaweed wraps are said to detoxify and increase blood circulation.

enveloppement de boue
mud wrap
Visit the spa for a relaxing massage, mud wrap, seaweed wrap or green tea herbal wrap.

envelopper
to wrap

épilation
hair removal
Medi-spas are facilities that traditionally offer beauty treatments such as facials, massages and hair removal, but they are increasingly offering medical procedures.

exfoliant / gommage
scrub

gommage du corps
body scrub

exfolier / gommer
to exfoliate / to scrub
A therapeutic bath gently exfoliates the skin and enhances circulation, leaving the skin feeling soft.

fontaine (d'eau potable)
drinking fountain
Llandrindod Wells, Wales, has springs rich in salt and iron and you can sample these waters at the drinking fountain in Rock Park.
At Leamington spa, the town's mineral drinking fountain is just outside the 19th century Royal Pump Rooms.

forme
fitness
Our fitness centre promotes a natural approach to fitness and well-being. You will find what you are looking for to enhance your health and improve your fitness levels.

forme (être en)
to be fit / to be in shape / to be in trim
He felt relaxed and fit after his holiday.

Why not try thalassotherapy? It will put you in trim!

rester en forme
to keep fit

en pleine forme
as fit as a fiddle

guérir
to cure / to heal
Thermal treatments do not cure at once, but they allow a reduction in medicine consumption.

guérison
healing

habitudes alimentaires
eating habits
Do you have healthy eating habits?

huile
oil

huile d'amande douce
sweet almond oil

huiles essentielles
essential oils
Some essential oils are used for aromatherapy while others are used for massage.

huile de massage
massage oil

hydrothérapie
hydrotherapy / aquatherapy
Hydrotherapy is one of the oldest health treatments. It involves the use of water for soothing pains and treating diseases.

kinésithérapeute
physical therapist

institut de beauté
beauty salon / beauty parlour

maigrir / perdre du poids
to lose weight
We will give you expert advice on exercise and nutrition to improve health, promote wellbeing and help you to lose weight and maintain your weight loss.

perte de poids
weight loss

masque facial
face mask

A regenerating face mask is ideal for wrinkles, blemishes and impurities.

massage
massage
Massages relax, stimulate lymph flow and blood circulation, relieve muscle, joint and ligament tension. They also help to treat neuralgic pains, arthritis, rheumatism, headaches, migraines and premenstrual syndrome.
Combined with the therapeutic qualities of essential oils, a massage can be a very invigorating or deeply relaxing experience.

salle de massage et de soins
massage room
We use all natural body products, organic cotton blankets, soft fleece pads on heated tables in comfortable massage rooms equipped with soft lighting and soothing music.

masser
to massage
To massage the body from head to toe.

masseur
masseur

médicinal
medicinal
The camomile plant is cultivated mainly for its medicinal properties.

herbes / plantes médicinales
medicinal herbs / medicinal plants

nutrition
nutrition

obèse
obese
Obese people are at greatly increased risk from a wide range of conditions, including diabetes, heart disease, strokes and certain cancers.

obésité
obesity
Health experts have warned that obesity is rising to epidemic proportions.
Obesity is a major killer.

indice de masse corporelle (IMC)
body mass index (BMI)
Obesity is measured using the Body Mass Index (BMI), which is a person's weight in kilogrammes divided by their height in metres squared. A BMI of 20 to 25 is normal, more than 25 is overweight and more than 30 is defined as obese.

piscine
pool / swimming pool
The open-air pools are fed by a radioactive thermal spring which flows at a constant temperature.

poids
weight

être en surpoids
to be overweight
General Practioners advise overweight patients to slim.

peser (se)
to weigh (oneself)

programme de remise en forme
fitness programme
Healthy cuisine, professional treatments, and fitness programmes are designed to enhance health and well-being.

régime
diet
The Kneipp cure, practised in German spas, consists of hydrotherapy, exercise, diet and relaxation.
The Mediterranean diet is well-balanced, full of foods which contain beneficial vitamins and minerals – in particular antioxidants which help to keep tissues healthy.

régime équilibré
balanced diet
Eating a balanced diet is important for maintaining good health and preventing illnesses.

régime hypolipidique / régime pauvre en graisses
low-cholesterol diet / low-fat diet
Up to now, low-fat diets, exercise programmes and drugs that suppress the appetite have been the main methods used to combat obesity.

régime hyposodé / régime sans sel
low-salt diet / salt-free diet

suivre un regime
to be on a diet

repos
rest
This spa is a peaceful oasis devoted to rest and relaxation.

se reposer
to rest

revitalisant
rejuvenating
Come and experience the magic of the healing mineral waters and rejuvenating spa treatments. You can drink our rejuvenating spa water and take a bath in it every morning.

revitaliser
to rejuvenate

rhumatismes
rheumatism

perclus de rhumatismes
crippled with rheumatism

rides
wrinkles / lines

combler les rides
to smooth out wrinkles / lines
The use of Botox is becoming increasingly popular in the UK as a treatment to smooth out wrinkles.

effacer les rides
to eradicate lines / wrinkles

sain
healthy
Healthy food.

santé
health
What better use of leisure than to improve one's health?
The character of spas has gradually changed as pleasure rather than health became the motivation for visitors.

en bonne santé
healthy / in good health (≠ unhealthy)

salle de remise en forme
fitness room

salon de coiffure
hair parlour

sauna
sauna / steamroom
Perhaps the best way to relax is to just close your eyes and surrender to the cleansing power of heat in a sauna.

soin du visage
facial (n)
Facial usually includes massaging, cleansing, toning, steaming, exfoliating and moisturizing.

soulager
to relieve / to ease away
To ease away aches and pains.
Mud baths relieve pain and fatigue and are used in treatments for rheumatic diseases.

soulagement
relief
Used in drinks and inhalations, the waters of Mont Dore give immediate relief to cure-takers.

source
spa / spring
Cheltenham's spa waters, which stem from a spring near the site of the town's ladies' college, were discovered in the 18th century.
The gushing springs of Desert Hot Springs – which can reach temperatures of 207 °F – are cooled to under 110 °F for therapeutic and recreational uses.
The springs of Baden-Baden have been enticing people to the western foothills of the Black Forest since Roman times.

source minérale
mineral spring
Vichy, dotted with extinct volcanoes, is rich in mineral springs.

sources thermales
thermal springs
Bath's unique thermal springs have been central in the city's history and development as one of the most famous spa towns in UK.
In Matlock Bath Derbyshire, warm thermal springs produce water at a temperature of 20 °C.

station climatique
health resort

station thermale
spa / spa-town / spa resort
Vittel is a lively spa resort. It is a heaven for those seeking physical and spiritual renewal.
The Romans transformed Bath into England's finest spa resort naming it after a native celtic goddess, Aquae Sulis.

thalassothérapie
thalassotherapy
Thalassotherapy remains fairly upmarket.

institut / centre de thalassothérapie
thalassotherapy centre

Thalassotherapy centres offer a range of specialised treatments for both men and women to relax, rejuvenate and re-balance the body.

thérapeutique (adj)
therapeutic
The thermal water therapeutic qualities have been renowned for a long time.

thérapie
therapy

thermalisme
spa tourism / thermal tourism
Spa tourism used to be the preserve of older, well-heeled women who went to spas for beauty treatments or to lose weight. Spas are now appealing to a younger less affluent clientele.
The International Congress on Thermal Tourism was held in the tiny spa-town of Mondariz in Northern Spain.

thermal
thermal
Nieuweschans, a charming fortified village, is both an international thermal spa and a modern thermal complex.

thermes
thermae
Evian's thermae are one of the best places to cure liver and stomach troubles.

tisane
herbal tea
Fruit and herbal teas have been proven to have many benefits to mind and body.
Sip on organic herbal tea while relaxing in the quiet room before or after your massage.

tourisme médical
medical tourism
Medical tourism is the act of travelling to other countries to obtain medical, dental and surgical treatment.
Epidauria was the sanctuary of the healing god Asklepios. It became the original travel destination for health and medical tourism.

tourisme de santé
health tourism
Health tourism is travel to improve one's health, such as a visit to a health resort or weight-loss camp.

traitement
treatment

What are your most popular treatments?
The Indian government hopes to encourage medical tourism, selling foreigners the idea of travelling for low-cost but world-class medical treatment.
These waters are particularly recommended for the treatment of metabolic ailments.

traiter
to treat
Spa therapy and balneotherapy may be effective for treating patients with low back pain.

trouble / affection
disorder

troubles alimentaires
eating disorders
Eating disorders such as anorexia, bulimia and binge eating have become major health problems.

troubles circulatoires
circulation disorders / blood circulation disorders

troubles dermatologiques
skin disorders
Acne, psoriasis and eczema are skin disorders.

troubles digestifs
bowel disorders / digestive disorders

troubles hépatiques
liver disorders

troubles rénaux
kidney disorders

troubles rhumatismaux
rheumatic disorders
Is spa therapy cost-effective in rheumatic disorders?

troubles veineux / insuffisance veineuse chronique
venous problems / vein problems / chronic venous insufficiency
60 to 70 % of patients treated in spa resorts, specialising in vascular diseases, have venous problems.
Venous problems may cause leg discomfort, leg swelling.
Vein problems affect both men and women.

RESTAURATION
The catering industry

1
GASTRONOMIE
Gastronomy
---

addition
bill / check (US) / tab (US)
Could we have the bill please?
Could you bring us the bill please?

payer l'addition
to foot the bill / to pay the bill

aigre-doux
sweet and sour
Sweet and sour is a combination of flavours usually found in Chinese cooking (sweet and sour chicken / sweet and sour pork…).

amuse-gueule
appetizer
Our new expanded menu offers a large assortment of appetizers including crabmeat cocktail, shrimps and oysters.

appétissant
appetizing (≠ unappetizing)

assaisonnement
dressing / seasoning

assaisonner
to season

vinaigrette
French dressing / salad dressing

auberge
inn / country inn
We stopped at a cosy historic inn specialising in Irish stew, Celtic steaks and fresh seafood.

aubergiste
innkeeper

boissons
beverages / drinks

boissons alcoolisées
alcoholic drinks

boissons non alcoolisées
soft drinks

boissons gazeuses
carbonated drinks / fizzy drinks

bon appétit
enjoy your meal!

buffet
buffet
On Fridays, try our all-you-can-eat seafood buffet!
Hot food buffet.
A Chinese buffet restaurant in San Francisco.

café
coffee

café filtre
filter coffee

cappuccino
cappuccino

expresso
expresso

café noir
black coffee

café crème
white coffee / coffee with cream

décaféiné
decaffeinated

carte
menu
What's on the menu?
This restaurant specialises in fish and its menu includes dishes such as sea bass, salmon…

manger à la carte
to eat à la carte

renouveller
to change

Our restaurant menu regularly changes. This reflects the seasons and the availability of the best produce.

casse-croûte
snack

client
customer / diner (restaurant) / guest / patron (pub)
Diners described the food as superb but pricey.
Diners can watch their specialties being prepared in ovens, broilers or deep-fryers.

habitués
regulars

commande
order
Can I take your order?
Last orders please!

commander
to order
Are you ready to order?

copieux
substantial
A substantial meal.

crème / crème fraîche
cream

crème anglaise
custard

crème fouettée / Chantilly
whipped cream
Buns, scones and muffins are served with whipped cream and homemade strawberry preserves.

crêpes
pancakes / French crêpes
In the UK, pancake races form an important part of the Shrove Tuesday celebration – an opportunity for large numbers of people to race down the streets tossing pancakes.
The French crêpe is thin and crispy. A crêpe Suzette is folded and heated in a sauce of butter, sugar, orange juice and liqueur.
American pancakes are also called battercake, griddlecakes or flapjacks.

crêpes salées
savoury pancakes
Savoury pancakes with ham, mushroom or cheese filling.

crêpes sucrées
sweet pancakes

crustacés
shellfish

cuisine (activité)
cooking

cuisine (art culinaire)
cuisine
When in Taormina, try the excellent local cuisine. They make sure to sample the local cuisine wherever they travel.

cuisine du terroir
country-style cooking
Country-style cooking is drawing on regional dishes and ingredients.

grande cuisine
haute cuisine
This restaurant is renowned for its haute cuisine.

nouvelle cuisine
"nouvelle cuisine"
Bernard Loiseau was famous for his "nouvelle cuisine", which sought to maximise simple flavours and reduce the use of heavy sauces.

cuisiner
to cook / to do the cooking

cuisinier
cook

chef cuisinier
chef
A leading French chef has been asked to help create space food for astronauts on long-term voyages in space.

débarasser la table
to clear the table

déjeuner / dîner (vb)
to have lunch / to have dinner

déjeuner de qqch / dîner de
to lunch on sth / to lunch off sth / to dine on sth / to dine off sth

dessert
dessert / pudding / sweet
What's for pudding?
For dessert try the Key Lime Pie.

dresser la table
to lay the table / to set up the table

eau
water

eau gazeuse / pétillante
sparkling water / carbonated water / fizzy water

eau minérale
mineral water

eau plate
still water

emporter
to take away / to take out
I'd like a hamburger to take out.

plat à emporter
take-away / take-out
A take away pizza.

repas à emporter
take-away meal / take-away food

entrée / hors d'œuvre
starter / hors d'œuvre / appetizer
Smoked salmon pâté is a traditional Irish starter.
The new expanded menu offers a large assortment of appetizers including crabmeat cocktail, shrimps and oysters.

épices
spices
Saffron is the most expensive spice in the world. It gives a distinctive aroma and yellow colour to Spanish paella. It is also a classic ingredient in the French fish soup bouillabaisse.

épicé
spicy
Food such as curry or chilli is usually hot and spicy.
If you like spicy food, then you will love Mexican cuisine because most dishes are packed with spices and chillies.

étoile
star
Three stars are awarded to top-rate restaurants. For the first time, France's Michelin restaurant guide has given its top three-star ranking to a woman chef.

restaurants étoilés par le Guide Michelin
Michelin star listed restaurants

gagner une étoile au Guide Michelin
to be awarded a Michelin star / to win a Michelin star / to gain a Michelin star

The restaurant was awarded a Michelin star last year.
Michelin awarded one star to five more London restaurants but not a single establishment gained a second or third star.

formule (restaurant)
fixed-price meal

fromage
cheese
A selection of French cheeses.

plateau de fromages
cheese board

fruits de mer
seafood
If you want to enjoy local fresh seafood, this is the place for you. Expertise in the kitchen and a warm and friendly atmosphere in the restaurant awaits you.

plateau de fruits de mer
seafood platter
Could we have a seafood platter for two?

gastronomie
gastronomy

gastronome
gastronome / gourmet

gastronomique
gourmet / gastronomic
South Africa's reputation as a gourmet destination has increased in the past decade.
Lyons is the gastronomic capital of France.

circuit gastronomique
food and drink trail
The number of food and drink trails has multiplied in Britain (sausage trails in the Midlands and the North-West, Lake District afternoon tea trail, etc.).

guide gastronomique
dining guide / dining directory / food and restaurant guide / restaurant directory
Dining guides like the Good Food Guide or Michelin Red Guide are widely recognized and influential guides across Europe.

tourisme gastronomique
gastro-tourism / food tourism / gourmet tourism
With British cuisine no longer a national joke, food tourism is booming.

Food tourism is growing in the USA. An increasing number of vacationers are basing their travel around food and wine.
Gourmet tourism is increasingly popular in France.

goûter / déguster
to sample / to taste / to try
Try Cheshire cheese, a crumbly salty cheese with a nutty flavour.

grill
grill / steak-house
The Spyglass grill is a great spot for a snack while claiming a bird's-eye view of the 9th green of Spyglass Hill golf course.

insipide
tasteless

inviter qqn au restaurant
to wine and dine somebody

jardin
garden

jardin aménagé sur le toit
roof garden

jardin d'un pub
beer garden

jus de fruits
fruit juices

légumes
vegetables

livre de cuisine
cookbook / cookery book
The Thanksgiving cookbook.
Jamie Oliver's cookbooks include Jamie's Kitchen, Jamie's Dinners, Cook with Jamie…

recettes
recipes
"Tea Time" was founded by Jane Pettigrew. The many varieties of tea are accompanied by cakes and pastries made following the original recipes found in Jane Pettigrew's book.

menu
set menu / fixed price meal
Do you have a set menu?

menu gastronomique
gourmet menu

menu du terroir
regional menu

menu touristique
tourist menu

mode de cuisson
way of cooking

bouillir
to boil

cuire à la vapeur
to steam

cuire au four
to bake

frire
to fry

faire sauter
to stir-fry

griller
to grill / to broil

rôtir
to roast

nourriture
food / fare / grub
Holidaymakers want food which emphasises the heritage and culture of a place.
Many of CapeTown's premier restaurants are situated on wine estates, where the best local wines complement fine fare.

nourriture servie dans les pubs
pub food / pub grub

s'offrir / se payer qqch
to treat oneself to sthg

c'est moi qui régale
this is my treat!

panier repas
packed lunch
Packed lunches will be handed out prior to each departure from your hotel.

panier pique-nique
picnic basket

plat / mets
dish
Many regional dishes are named after a county such as Lancashire hotpot, Cornish pasties…
Typical American dishes include clam chowder, southern fried chicken, pecan pie and hash browns.

plat d'accompagnement
side dish

plat du jour
today's special

plats cuisinés
ready-cooked dishes

plats surgelés
frozen food

plat / partie du repas
course
A three-course meal.

plat de résistance / plat principal
main course

plat de poisson / plat de viande
fish course / meat course

repas avec entrée, plat et dessert
three-course meal

poisson
fish

pourboire
tip / gratuity (US)
Restaurant waiters normally get a tip of around 10 % of the bill.

pourboire compris
tip included

laisser un pourboire
to tip / to give a tip / to leave a tip
A recent survey found out that customers at London restaurants were the least generous when it came to tips, leaving the waiter the equivalent of 12 % of the bill, compared with 18 % in New York.
Tipping is not expected in fast food restaurants.

pourcentage pour le service
gratuity
We were charged a 12 % gratuity.

proposer
to feature
Many restaurants feature an early bird menu.
The menu features international as well as American specialties.

recommander
to recommend

recommandé
recommended
This country inn is highly recommended and much praised by all guests.

réservation recommandée
advance reservation advised

renommé / réputé
celebrated / famed / famous / renowned / well-known
Located just two minutes away from Hyde Park, Brown's is well known for its afternoon teas.

repas
meal
Meals are served on the terrace overlooking the lake.
On average, Londoners eat or take away nearly half of their meals.

repas d'affaires
business lunch

repas traditionnel du dimanche (UK)
roast dinner / Sunday roast / Sunday roast dinner
A roast dinner typically includes roast beef with fresh vegetables, plenty of gravy and Yorkshire puddings.

repas indien
Indian dinner

petit déjeuner anglais
full English breakfast

petit déjeuner continental
continental breakfast

pause café
tea break / coffee break

brunch
brunch (breakfast + lunch on Sundays)

déjeuner
lunch

goûter
afternoon snack / afternoon tea
The hotel serves afternoon teas.
Why not enjoy an afternoon tea including sandwiches, cakes, scones and tea?

dîner
dinner

dîner avant spectacle
pre-theatre supper

prendre un repas
to have a meal / to take a meal

se mettre à table
to sit down to a meal

restaurant
restaurant / eatery / eating place
There is a large Bangladeshi community in east London and many restaurants with an Indian theme.

cafétéria / self
cafeteria / self-service restaurant

bar à salades
salad bar
Many modern attractive healthy lunch spots and salad bars have opened up lately.
An "all-you-can-eat" salad bar.

snack-bar / petit resto
café / caff / snack-bar / diner
Three quarters of customers say that they want to see local foods named on restaurant and café menus, in particular vegetables, meat and poultry.
Mrs Bumbles Tea Room was voted Rochester's best café.

restaurant branché
trendy restaurant / trendy eatery
It is the latest trendy restaurant to have opened on the square.

restaurant gastronomique
gourmet restaurant

restaurant végétarien
vegetarian restaurant

restauroute
diner

aller au restaurant
to go to a restaurant / to eat out / to have a meal out / to dine out

restaurateur
restaurateur / restaurant owner

restauration rapide
fast food
Traditional fast food such as burgers and chips will compete with low-fat alternatives.

fast food / restaurant rapide
fast food restaurant / quick service restaurant (QSR)
Mac Donald's is the world's largest chain of fast food restaurants.
Fast food restaurants offer both counter service and drive-through service.

salon de thé
coffee-shop / tea-room / tea shop

The Earl Grey Tea Rooms in York supply teas from all over the world.
Oxfam is to launch a chain of fair trade coffee shops in Britain.
The hotel has a cosy coffee-shop on the ground floor where you can sip coffee and snacks are served all day.

savoureux
tasty

servir
to serve
Fast food restaurants serve all sorts of delicacies from American style hamburgers, hot dogs and fried chicken to Italian pizza, Mexican tacos and Chinese egg rolls.
Traditional tea is served every afternoon in the comfortable, intimate surroundings of this charming hotel, which is located right across the street from the Metropolitan Museum.

servir à table
to wait at table

service
service
Service is fast and courteous and the atmosphere pleasant.
Flawless service and excellent pastries make this tea room a real "must-do" for tea aficionados.

service de premier ordre / impeccable
service is second to none / flawless / impeccable

premier / second service
first / second sitting

serveur
waiter

chef de rang / maître d'hôtel
head waiter / maître d'hôtel

tarte / tourte
pie
minced pies / steak-and-kidney pie / chicken pie / apple pie

table d'hôte (menu à prix fixe)
table d'hôte
The table d'hôte menu offers good value.
Enjoy a Bridget Jones's Diary Package, consisting of a two-night stay in a suite, a chilled bottle of Chardonnay and a platter of chocolate-dipped strawberries on arrival, three-course table d'hôte dinner and full English breakfast.

ticket restaurant
luncheon voucher (LV)

Luncheon vouchers are accepted in over 333,000 outlets in the UK and used by over 100,000 people every month in cafes, sandwich bars and restaurants.

accepter / prendre les tickets restaurants
to accept luncheon vouchers

In a competitive market, more and more restaurants, food outlets and retailers are seeing the advantages of accepting luncheon vouchers.

viande
meat

crue
raw

bleue
very rare

saignante
rare / underdone

à point
medium

bien cuite
well-done

pas assez cuite
undercooked

trop cuite
overcooked

How would you like your burger? rare, medium or well-done?

à volonté
unlimited

The seafood supper on Friday and Saturday nights is excellent value as "unlimited wine" is included.

nourriture à volonté
all-you-can-eat

An all-you-can-eat buffet of sweets.

——— 2 ———
VINS ET SPIRITUEUX
Wines and spirits

amateur de vins
wine lover / wine connoisseur

Clos Pegase has become a pilgrimage for wine lovers.

Thousands of wine lovers are expected to visit South Africa's vineyards.

accorder les mets et les vins
to pair food and wine / to match food and wine / to harmonize food and wine

accord mets / vins
food and wine pairing

A food and wine pairing guide.

appellation
appellation

appellation d'origine contrôlée (AOC)
appellation d'origine contôlée / American Viticultural Area appellation (AVA appellation) / guaranteed vintage

The Bureau of Alcohol, Tobacco and Firearms (BATF) established the American equivalent to AOC – the AVA appellation – to certify wine growing regions in the USA.

The AOC label for champagne covers vineyards in 319 villages spread out across 83,000 acres in north-eastern France.

bar / pub
public bar / pub / boozer (fam.)

The tradition of games like darts is largely retained in British pubs.

The social hub of Irish life is the pub, with its own unique charm.

The loss of a community pub can have a negative impact on the local economy and tourism.

bar à vins
wine bar

Wine bars have started to replace some of the pubs.

The best London wine bars combine atmosphere with an in-depth knowledge about wine.

bière
beer

bière blonde
lager

bière brune
brown ale

bière brune avec mousse (type Guinness)
stout

bière pression
draught beer / draft beer / beer on tap

bière rousse
bitter

bière sans alcool
alcohol-free beer

un demi
half a pint / half a pint of lager

un demi panaché
half a lager shandy

boire à la santé de qqn
to drink to somebody's health / to drink a toast to so

à votre santé / à la vôtre
your health / good health / cheers

bouchon
cork

goût de bouchon / bouchonné
corked
The waiter returned a bottle of Cabernet Sauvignon to the kitchen because the wine was corked.

bouteille de vin
bottle of wine

cuvée spéciale
special bottling / reserve

cuvée du patron (restaurant)
house wine

carte des vins
wine-list
A comprehensive wine list.
Would you like to see the wine-list Sir?
Restaurants pay close attention to their wine lists, looking over what wines are available on the market and tailoring their selections to compliment the restaurant's cuisine.

vins au verre
wines by the glass
The wine list offers over 2,000 selections, including over 50 wines by the glass.
The list has been divided into three sections, the Market List, the Reserve List and the By the Glass List.

cave
cellar
This state-of-the-art cellar has the capacity to produce around 70,000 cases. The cellar also boasts a viniteque, where bottled wines can be kept under ideal conditions until ready to be enjoyed.

cave de négociant-éléveur
wine cellar

visite des caves
wine cellar tour
Wine cellar tours last about 1hour and include wine tasting.

cépages
varietals / wine-type grapes / grape varieties
White varietals include Sauvignon Blanc, Riesling, Chardonnay, etc.
Red varietals include Pinot Noir, Cabernet Sauvignon, Merlot, Shiraz, etc.

cépages blancs
white varietals

cépages rouges
red varietals

champagne
champagne.
France is planning to expand the area in which wine growers are allowed to make champagne, in a bid to cope with growing demand for the luxury drink.
Prosecco, Italy's cheaper alternative to champagne is gaining in popularity.

une coupe de champagne
a glass of champagne
The waiter poured them both a glass of champagne.

cidre
cider
England and Wales are traditional cider makers. To make cider, use good quality fruit, then press the apples and let the juices ferment in oak barrels for about eight months.

cognac
brandy / burnt wine
They sipped brandy after the meal.

concours de vins
wine competition
It doesn't matter how well a wine is doing in the market place, it still has to stand up to the fierce test of wine competitions.

vins médaillés
award-winning wines / medal winning wines
They produce a wide range of award winning premium quality wines available worldwide.

cuve
tank

déboucher une bouteille
to uncork a bottle / to open a bottle

tire-bouchon
cork-screw
The Museum of the cork-screw at Menerbes in the Luberon boasts a thousand individual, hand-crafted cork-screws, the oldest dating from the 17th century.

dégustation de vins
wine-tasting / wine-sampling
Why not go on a course on the etiquette of wine-tasting?
Tasting is complimentary and occurs within a working winery amidst the barrels, crushers, tanks and presses.
Daily wine-tasting, cellar tours and sales are offered at most cellars. The tasters sip, swirl and spit the wines.

dégustation à l'aveugle
blind tasting
The US has emerged victorious in a blind tasting by experts in London and California pitting US and French wine against each other.

caveau de dégustation
tasting cellar
Wine may be tasted and bought at the tasting cellar at the entrance of the estate.

déguster
to taste / to sample
Some 3,5 million people visit the bucolic Napa and Sonoma valleys each year, primarily to watch the wine-making process and sample the results.

bouquet / nez
flavour / bouquet
One important wine-tasting skills is the ability to recognise the flavours that are encountered.

arôme de fruits rouges / baies
red fruit flavour / berry aroma
This wine has a distinct bouquet and characteristic red fruit flavour.

robe
colour
The wine of Cahors has a bright often deep red colour. It is a tannic wine very full in the mouth.

corps
body

vin léger
light-bodied wine

vin corsé
strong-bodied wine

vin charpenté / vin qui a du corps
full-bodied wine

vin tanique
tannic wine

digestif
after-dinner liqueur

distillerie
distillery
A guide will take you around the distillery and share some of the secrets of whisky production.
Visit the Glenfiddish Distillery still owned and managed by the Grant Family.

domaine viticole / propriété viticole
winery / winery estate / wine estate
Groot Constantia Estate is the oldest wine estate in South Africa, and it is here that the country's thriving wine industry has its roots.
The Paso Robles wine growing region is located half way between San Francisco and Los Angeles. The 24 square mile territory encompasses more than 26,000 vineyard acres and nearly 100 wineries.

étiquette
label
Nearly half of the British drinkers surveyed said they preferred to buy wine with a clear, modern label that listed basic information such as grape variety.

étiqueter
to label
The French have recently overturned centuries of tradition by allowing wine makers to label wine by grape and not region alone if they want.
The top chateaux, however, are continuing to use the Appellation d'Origine Contrôlée labelling system – a guarantee the wine has come from a specific geographical location.

foire aux vins
wine fair
The London International Wine Fair (LIWF) is an important event. For importers, merchants, producers, restaurateurs and sommeliers no other event offers the same opportunity to taste, meet

with suppliers and winemakers and get down to business as the LIWF.

fût
barrel / cask
To be called Scotch, the whisky must have been distilled in Scotland, aged in wooden barrels in Scotland for at least three years.

fûts neufs
new barrels

fûts de chêne
oak barrels / oak casks

élevé en fûts de chêne
aged in oak barrels

glaçon
ice-cube

goûter le vin
to taste the wine
The person who ordered the wine will usually be asked to taste it.

mettre en bouteilles
to bottle

mise en bouteilles
bottling

mis en bouteilles au domaine / à la propriété
estate bottled

millésime / année
vintage
What vintage is this wine?
In Bordeaux, recent vintages have been acclaimed, following a succession of warm summers.
This vintage is ready to drink now but it will improve with further bottle age.

une bonne année / un bon millésime
a vintage year
Wine growers in France are predicting a vintage year.
Europe's wine-growers are hoping for a vintage year as the exceptional summer heatwave has forced an early harvest.

vins millésimés
vintage wines
Vintage wines are made from grapes of a single year's harvest and are accordingly dated.

négociant en vins
wine merchant / vintner

Australian premium wines are available from selected wine merchants all over the world.

porto
port

produire du vin / faire du vin
to produce wine / to make wine
It is down south in the Cape, where climatic and topographic conditions simulate those of the old wine countries that South Africa's finest wines are produced.
The 10-acre vineyard produces about 35,000 bottles of red, white and sparkling wine each year.

pays producteur de vins
wine-producing country

propriétaire-récoltant
vineyard owner

récolte
harvest
This year the wine harvest could be the lowest in a decade after a summer of storms and heatwaves.

région vinicole
wine region / wineland / wine-growing region
Burgundy is one of France's most prestigious wine regions.
The Napa Valley in California is North America's most renowned wine-growing region.

route des vins
wine route
Stellenbosch Wine Route is one of the biggest tourist attraction in the Western Cape.

faire la route des vins
to go on a wine tasting tour

route du whisky
whisky trail / malt whisky trail
The malt whisky trail lies by the River Spey among the northern foothills of the Grampians.
The whisky trail will take you meandering through eight famous malt whisky distilleries in and around the Spey Valley.

faire la route du whisky
to tour the whisky trail

rhum
rum

servir le vin
to serve wine

At what temperature should wine be served?
Red wine should be served at room temperature
while white wine should be served chilled.

servir frais
to serve chilled

servir chambré
to serve at room temperature

sol
soil
California is blessed with the multiple micro-
climates and rich soils that produce very fine
Chardonnays, Cabernets and Zinfandels.

sommelier
wine waiter / sommelier
Part of the sommelier's role is to put together a
wine list that matches the restaurant's food and
the requirements of its clientele.

spiritueux
spirits

terroir
terroir

tournée
round / round of drinks

c'est ma tournée
it's my round

c'est la tournée du patron
the drinks are on the house

tournée des bars
pub crawl
If you are planning a night out or a pub crawl,
check the London pub guide, listing hundreds
of pubs!

vendanges
grape harvest / grape-picking / grape-gathering

vendanges tardives
late harvest
Late harvest Riesling.
California provides the vast majority of late
harvest dessert wines, blessed as it is with a
dry, lengthy harvest season.

vendanger / faire les vendanges
to pick the grapes / to harvest the grapes /
to gather the grapes

vieillissement / maturation
ageing / aging / maturing

faire vieillir un vin
to mature a wine / to age a wine
Oak casks are used to mature wines.
Fermenting or ageing white wines in oak
barrels gives the wine a wonderful whiff of
vanilla and spice.

vigneron / viticulteur
wine-grower / wine-maker
Napa Valley wine-growers believe their proximity
to the Pacific coast may protect them from the
worst effects of climate change.
Wine-makers are encouraging vineyard tourism.
Wine-makers in England said a change in tempe-
rature meant conditions in Kent and Sussex were
now more favourable to produce the grapes used
for Champagne.

viticulture
wine growing / wine farming industry
They have published a leaflet outlining the
history of wine growing in South Africa.

tourisme viticole
vineyard tourism
Vineyard tourism is catching on! There are
vineyard tours and visits to wineries and the
promise of gourmet food in restful surroun-
dings.

vignoble
vineyard
Grapes that produce good wine cost a premium so
getting the right conditions for good growth can
mean the difference between profit and loss for
small vineyards.
The vineyard is spread over a hill and growing
conditions are very different at the top and bottom
of the slope.

vin
wine

blanc / rosé / rouge
white / rosé / red

vin de cépage
varietal wine

vin bio
organic wine

vin demi-sec
medium dry wine

vin doux
sweet wine

vin sec
dry wine

vin de table
table wine
Table wines will now be encouraged to market themselves by grape variety or brand to make it easier for customers to choose wines.

vin effervescent / vin mousseux
sparkling wine
A sparkling wine made in Cornwall has won a gold medal.

vin chaud
mulled wine
What could be better than coming in from the cold to the spicy aroma of mulled wine?

vinification
winemaking
He oversees all aspects of winemaking.

vinifier
to make wine

whisky
whisky / whiskey

xérès
sherry
Dry sherry has become more fashionable and is being drunk as a refreshing chilled aperitif or an accompaniment to Spanish food.

TOURISME D'AFFAIRES
Business tourism

affaires
business

carrière dans les affaires
business career

carte de visite professionnelle
business card

centre d'affaires
business centre
The European Quality Alliance is planning to open fully equipped business centres throughout Eastern Europe.
This business centre has individual cubicles with phones and computer hookups, conference and VIP rooms and an area for copying, faxing and shredding.

classe affaires
business class / executive class
Business class passengers receive all the time-and-hassle-saving advantages of privileged check-in and priority baggage handling.

déjeuner d'affaires
business lunch

faire des affaires / travailler (avec qn)
to do business (with sb)
"Kiss, Bow or Shake Hands: How to Do Business in Sixty Countries" by Terri Morrison

femme d'affaires / homme d'affaires
businesswoman / businessman

femmes / homme d'affaires chevronnés
seasoned business people

femme / homme en voyage d'affaires
business traveller
Hotels are investing heavily in new technology aimed at improving and simplifying the stay of the business traveller.

monde des affaires
business world

rendez-vous d'affaires
business appointment
Fax machines and such amenities as chauffeur-driven limousines for business appointments are examples of the Ritz's aim of running a few years ahead of the competition in hotel services.

salon « affaires » (aéroport)
business lounge / business class lounge

voyages d'affaires (sens géneral)
business travel (unc) / executive travel
Business travel has gained a high degree of importance in the late eighties.
The Tapei International Convention Centre is sure to put Taiwan more firmly on the international business travel map.

voyage d'affaires
business trip

voyager pour affaires
to go on a business trip / to make a business trip / to travel on business
When travelling on business, you won't fail to appreciate a comfortable lounge providing business facilities.

budget déplacements / budget voyages
travel budget
The company has recently slashed its travel budget.

être en déplacement pour affaires
to be away on business

cadres
executives / managerial staff
Madrid's Ritz Hotel at the hub of the Spanish capital provides a favourite stopover for executives.

cadres moyens
middle management

cadres supérieurs
senior executives / top executives / top management / upper management

contrat
contract / deal
The company won a contract to build 50 planes.

conclure un contrat
to clinch a deal / to strike a deal
He was in Hungary, trying to clinch a deal for his employer.

distractions
entertainment

durer
to last
The International Conference on Urban Life will last five days.

entreprise
company / corporation / entreprise
The company develops, owns, manages or franchises hotels, resorts and vacation ownership properties.

équipement (services, confort)
amenities

équipement (infrastructure)
facilities
There are extensive conference facilities at the hotel including four large conference rooms and eight function rooms.

faciliter
to ease / to facilitate
Hotels are turning to new technology to ease business travel.

frais (n)
expenses / fee (s)

frais d'annulation
cancellation fee (s)

frais de déplacement
travelling expenses

frais d'inscription / droits d'inscription (congrès)
registration fees (convention)
Our records show that your registration fees still remain unpaid.

bénéficier d'une réduction / avoir droit à une réduction
to benefit from a discount / to be entitled to a discount
Students are entitled to a discount on conference registration fees.

couvrir (frais, dépenses)
to cover (expenses)
The local and travelling expenses will be covered by the company.

performant
efficient
High speed internet access will help business travellers be more efficient while travelling.

personnel (n)
personnel / staff
During conventions, a numerous staff must be hired.

personnel de restauration / de secrétariat / de traduction
catering staff / secretarial staff / translating staff

programme
programme / program (US)
We've just received the programme of social events.

programmer / plannifier
to plan

report
postponment

reporter
to postpone
The meeting has been postponed.

réservation
booking / reservation
Travel bookings are optimized around a traveller's preferences for airline flights, hotels and car rentals.

effectuer une réservation
to book / to make a reservation
Book early to avoid disappointment!

réunion
meeting
Due to circumstances beyond our control, the meeting has been cancelled.

être en réunion d'affaires
to be in a business meeting

réunion du Conseil d'Administration
Board Meeting
The Board Meeting will be held on Monday.

se réunir
to meet, to convene

salle de réunion
function room / meeting room

salon (foire, exposition)
exhibition / fair / trade-fair

Los Angeles County Fair features acres of home arts, floral and agricultural displays, plus livestock judging and wine competition.

salon (hôtel, aéroport)
lounge
Weary businessmen can sit and relax in the hotel lounge.

traitement de faveur
red-carpet treatment
Business travellers expect red carpet treatment (ex: welcomme cocktail, complimentary drinks…).

voyages de stimulation
incentive travel (uncount) / incentive trips
Incentive travel is travel given by firms to employees, dealers or distributors as a reward for some special endeavour or as a spur to achievement.
Incentive trips originated in the USA during the 1960s.

1
LES CONFÉRENCES / LES CONGRÈS
Conferences / Conventions
---

atelier
workshop
Four workshops offering a hands-on approach to ESP are planned.

auditorium
auditorium
The main auditorium seats 350 people and features built-in audio visual equipment.

commission, jury
panel

groupe d'experts, de spécialistes
panel of experts / think tank / task force

réunion-débat
panel discussion

communication
paper / presentation

faire une communication
to give a presentation / to make a presentation

He gave a presentation on the new economy.

présenter une communication
to present a paper

appel à communication
call for papers

conférence
conference
The 11th annual FT World Pharmaceuticals Conference, 21 & 22 June 2000, London.

conférencier
lecturer / speaker

salle de conférences (amphithéâtre)
conference theatre / lecture theatre
This hotel features a spectacular conference theatre perfect for state-of-the-art audiovisual presentations.

salle de conférence
conference room
Our conference rooms have a seating capacity of about 100 each.

conférence-vidéo
video-conference
Video-conferences can be a cheaper alternative to business trips since electronic sessions can accommodate as many participants as can fit in a studio.

congrès
congress / convention
A Teachers' Convention. A Doctors' Convention. Conventions can give a temporary boost to local employment.

congressiste
convention member / delegate / participant
The conference attracted some 150 delegates from more than 20 countries.

actes du congrès
conference proceedings
I was sent a copy of the conference proceedings.

palais des congrès
convention centre
This city boasts a multi-purpose convention centre with seating for over 600 delegates.

donner une conférence
to deliver a conference / a lecture
He delivered a fascinating lecture on breast reconstruction.

inscription
registration

bulletin d'inscription / formulaire d'inscription
registration form
Please fill in the registration form and send it back to the organizing committee at your earliest convenience.

date limite d'inscription
registration deadline

frais d'inscription
registration fee
A VAT receipt will be sent on payment of the registration fee.

s'inscrire
to register

langue de travail
working language
The working language of the conference will be French.

lieu
venue / site
Selecting the venue for a conference is more and more governed by the proximity of golfing facilities.
Enclosed are directions to the conference site.

avoir lieu
to be held / to take place
Please note that as the conference is being held in the UK all registrants are liable to pay UK VAT at 17.5%.
The next International Symposium on Plastic and Reconstructive Surgery will be held in Atlanta.
Many international conferences take place in Geneva.

organiser
to organize / to stage
The convention was staged by the American Society of Plastic and Reconstructive Surgeons.

organisateur
organizer
A conference organizer, a meeting organizer.

comité organisateur / comité d'organisation
planning committee / organizing committee / steering committee / steering group

participer à une conférence
to attend a conference
They attended a conference on macroeconomics.

participant
attendee
Internet access will be made available to all conference attendees.

participation
attendance
Attendance at the conference will be limited to 200.
Companies say that Internet access can boost productivity and attendance at business events.

président (d'un congrès, d'une réunion, d'une session)
chairman

présider
to chair (a convention, a meeting, a session...)

remplaçant
substitute delegate
Cancellations will be subject to a 20% cancellation fee unless a substitute delegate is offered.

secrétariat du congrès
conference secretariat
All correspondence referring to registration for the conference should be sent to the conference secretariat.

séminaire
seminar

sujet / question
issue

aborder un sujet
to examine an issue
The conference will examine issues from the need for new business models to the increasing emphasis on the use of new technologies to promote growth.

symposium (pl.: symposia)
symposium
The symposium language will be English.

thème
theme / topic
As the industry experiences yet more consolidation, the theme of this year's event will address the factors that drive the industry.

2

ÉQUIPEMENT POUR CONFÉFENCES
Conference facilities

In our purpose-built conference theatre a complete range of AV equipment is available for all functions.

accès internet
internet access
Hilton Hotels Corporation and CAIS internet have announced an agreement to offer premiere high speed internet access in Hilton hotels.

écouteur
earphone

écran
screen

écran de projection
projection screen

imprimante
printer
Hilton, Sheraton and Hyatt have installed printers and fax machines in business-class rooms.

lutrin
lectern

magnétophone
tape-recorder

magnétoscope
video-cassette-recorder (VCR)

matériel audio-visuel
audio-visual equipment (AV)

ordinateur portable
laptop computer
Guests may easily access the Internet with a laptop computer.

photocopieuse
photocopier / photocopying machine

prise pour ordinateur
computer hookup

projecteur de diapositives avec plateau et écran
slide projector with tray and screen

projecteur de films
film projector / movie projector (US)

rétroprojecteur
overhead projector (OHP)

service télécopie
fax service

supports visuels
visual aids

télécopieur
fax machine

traduction simultanée
simultaneous translation

transparents
view-graphs

vidéo projecteur
video projector

TOURISME DURABLE
Sustainable tourism

arrière-pays
backcountry / hinterland

They visited a tiny village somewhere in the hinterland of Portsmouth.

artisanat
crafts / craft industry

Just north of Windhoek you can find a wide selection of African crafts in the largest curio market in Namibia.

artisanat local
local handicrafts / locally-made handicrafts

Tourists are taken to Maasai areas to buy handicrafts and beadwork.

Purchase handicrafts to support the local economy using the principles of fair trade.

Encourage tourists to buy locally-made handicrafts and products.

produits artisanaux
artisanal products

UNESCO is specially involved in stimulating the creation of original models, in the promotion of quality handicrafts and in the commercialization of artisanal products on the international market.

association à but non lucratif
non-profit organization / not for profit organization

The Global Water Foundation is a non-profit organization dedicated to delivering clean water and sanitation to the world's neediest communities.

association humanitaire
humanitarian aid organization

atténuer
to mitigate

The negative environmental and social impacts of tourism can be mitigated with appropriate planning, management and monitoring of tourism activities.

authenticité
authenticity

Authenticity is the new buzzword. Wealthier western travellers are eschewing package tours for more exotic, individual experiences.

authentique
authentic

Some tour operators work directly with local people to make authentic cultural experiences more accessible and affordable to independent holidaymakers.

Many tourists are abandoning the mock-European high-rises for more authentic experiences in the bush.

autochtone
indigenous

The cultural resources of indigenous peoples are a fragile treasure that is now under threat from globalization.

populations autochtones / peuples autochtones
indigenous peoples

The fact that the cultures of indigenous peoples are in danger of dying out cannot fail to be a matter of concern.

savoirs autochtones
indigenous knowledge / traditional knowledge

Indigenous knowledge, also referred to as traditional knowledge, has emerged as a priority concern on the international environment and development agenda.

bénévole (n)
volunteer

Tourists who choose to spend their holidays working overseas with local communities and volunteer groups can gain life-enriching travel experiences whilst providing practical solutions through dedicating their skills and time.

besoins
needs

répondre aux besoins
to meet needs / to satisfy needs
Ecotourism in Sri Lanka is to be used as a tool to conserve the environment, to give maximum economic benefits to the host community, preserve age-old cultural heritage, and to satisfy the needs of ecotourists visiting genuine eco sites in the island.

biotope
habitat
Namibia has a broad range of mammals due to the diversity of its habitats.

chasse
hunting / shooting
The community is a mix of eight different Indian tribes. They still live from traditional hunting and fishing.
Conservation International has agreed with the community on a hunting zone and a no hunting zone to protect wildlife and biodiversity.

chassse aux grands fauves
big game hunting

permis de chasse
hunting licence / shooting licence

saison de chasse
hunting season / shooting season

chasser / aller à la chasse
to hunt / to go hunting

chasseur
huntsman / hunter

chasseur d'ivoire
ivory hunter

commerce
trade
Wildlife trade must be monitored and restricted.

communautés d'accueil
host communities
Host communities benefit from positive contributions to their natural, social and cultural environments and economic well-being.

communautés locales
local communities
Tourists are brought closer to the local communities.

compatible avec
consistent with
Tourism activities should be consistent with the principles of conservation and sustainable use of biological diversity.

contribuer à
to contribute to
The rush to "see it before it's gone" is hastening damage to the environment, encouraging tourists to take flights and other means of travel that contribute to greenhouse gas emissions.

croissance économique
economic growth
Tourism has an enormous capacity to provide much needed economic growth to developing countries.

coût
cost
The total cost of the project is estimated to be just under €1M.

coutumes
habits / customs
Always observe local customs!
Ecotourism encourages tourists to explore areas in small groups, staying in local accommodation, eating local food, observing local customs and culture.

déboisement
deforestation
We must preserve forests. Deforestation contributes to mud slides.

déchets
waste
Taking action on waste is essential, since we are consuming natural resources at an unsustainable rate and contributing unnecessarily to climate change.

recyclage des déchets
waste recycling

recycler les déchets
to recycle waste
The Government is hoping to increase the amount of household waste that we recycle to 33 % by 2015. Some of the materials that we can recycle include paper, plastics, metals (such as aluminium cans) and tyres.

dégradation / dégâts
degradation / damage
coastal degradation / environmental degradation

A particular concern is the degradation of biodiversity and fragile ecosystems such as coral reefs, mountains, coastal areas and wetlands.

WWF believes that all tourism must be planned and managed in a way that avoids damage to biodiversity and is environmentally sustainable, economically viable and socially equitable.

dégrader
to damage / to cause damage to / to degrade
Sustainable tourism uses tourist resources today in a way that does not damage them for future visitors and local people.

déplacement (de population)
displacement
An eco-tourism project is being criticised as it will cause the displacement of 25,000 indigenous people.

développement
development
Ecotourism propels development.

développement culturel
cultural development

développement socio-économique
socio-economic development
What's the impact of tourism on socio-economic development?

outils de développement
development tools
The promotion of ecotourism should be integrated into sustainable development tools such as land-use, mobility planning, economic and social planning at regional and local levels.

désertification
desertification

directives / principes directeurs
guidelines
Ecotourists should follow the recommended guidelines.

Here are some guidelines for tour operators working in environmentally-sensitive areas: make tourism and conservation compatible, support the preservation of wilderness and biodiversity, use natural resources in a sustainable way, minimize consumption, waste and pollution, respect local cultures, educate staff, follow safety rules...

dormir à la belle étoile
to sleep in the open / to sleep under the stars
Sleep under the stars with only the canvas walls of your tent separating you from the wild.

nuit étoilée
starlit night / starry night

droits de l'homme
human rights

durable
sustainable

consommation durable
sustainable consumption

développement durable
sustainable development
"Sustainable development is development that meets the needs of the present without compromising the ability of future generations to meet their own needs." Gro Harlem Brundtland, Our Common Future, *1992.*

tourisme durable
sustainable tourism
UNWTO plays a central and decisive role in promoting the development of responsible, sustainable and universally accessible tourism.

eau
water

eau courante
running water

eau potable
drinking water
The Global Water Foundation facilitates the provision of humanitarian aid throughout the developing world, with the ultimate goal of providing safe, healthy, drinking water and adequate sanitation in areas where it is not available.

non potable
unsafe to drink / unfit for drinking

approvisionnement en eau
water supply
Accessibility and water supply have been compromised.

approvisionner en eau
to supply water

échanges
exchanges

écologique
ecological / environmental
Removing rare plants and birds' eggs affects the ecological balance.
"We endorse this philosophy: take only pictures, leave only footprints" (Australian Environmental Policy).

écomusée
ecomuseum

écosystème
ecosystem
Tourism is a source of increasing stress on fragile ecosystems.
The natural ecosystems and biological resources that may be threatened by tourism development provide the very goods and services that underpin the tourism industry.

écotourime
ecotourism
Ecotourism in Africa varies widely. Tourists can view gorillas in Uganda and lemurs in Madagascar, go trekking in Ethiopia and birding in Botswana, look at rock paintings in South Africa, visit rainforests in Ghana, and enjoy walking and photographic safaris in Namibia.
Ecotourism involves a wide range of interest groups, from local communities and indigenous peoples to global corporations, national governments and development agencies.

écotouriste
ecotourist / eco-traveller
As an eco-traveller it is your responsibility to prevent or minimise any negative impacts on the environment, local community and economy of the destination you are visiting.

l'emploi
employment
Employment generated by ecotourism-related jobs is sometimes one of the most significant benefits for local communities, providing supplemental income to rural farmers, women and young people.

emplois
jobs
The project is expected to generate income for local people through ecotourism, investment opportunity and jobs.

création d'emplois
job creation

créer des emplois
to create jobs / to generate jobs
Sustainable tourism has the potential to create jobs.

engagement / implication
commitment / involvement

s'engager à / s'impliquer dans
to commit oneself to / to involve oneself in
We commit ourselves to pursue the principles of sustainable tourism.

enrichir
to enrich / to make richer
It will certainly enrich your travel experience!
Guides know about the plants, wildlife, history and folklore of the country – making holiday experiences much richer!

enrichissant
enriching

enrichissement
enrichment
Travel has to do with stimulus, enrichment and a sense of achievement.
The quest for cultural enrichment.

entrée interdite
no admittance / no entry / keep out

entreprendre
to undertake
They have undertaken conservation and tourism development projects in Africa.

équitable
fair

commerce équitable
fair trade

tourisme équitable
fair trade tourism / fair trade in tourism / fair tourism
Fair trade tourism is inspired by fair trade principles. It focuses more particularly on the participation of host communities in democratic decision making, in eco-friendly production systems and in fair wages for local services.
Travellers' demand for fair tourism experiences is increasing.

espèce
species

espèces menacées / espèces en voie de disparition
endangered species / species in danger of extinction / species on the brink of being wiped out
Do not buy products made from endangered plants or animals.
About 20 % of animal and plant species in China are in danger of extinction.

éthique (n)
ethics

code mondial d'éthique du tourisme
global code of ethics for tourism (GCET)
The Global Code of Ethics for Tourism is a comprehensive set of principles whose purpose is to guide stakeholders in tourism development: central and local governments, local communities, the tourism industry and its professionals, as well as visitors, both international and domestic.
The 10 point Global Code of Ethics for Tourism was approved unanimously by the UNWTO General Assembly meeting in Santiago in October 1999.

définir les règles du jeu
to outline the rules of the game
The Code includes nine articles outlining the "rules of the game" for destinations, governments, tour operators, developers, travel agents, workers and travellers themselves.
The tenth article involves the redress of grievances and marks the first time that a code of this type will have a mechanism for enforcement.

éthique (adj)
ethical
What are the ethical problems associated with tourism?

soulever des problèmes éthiques
to raise ethical questions / issues
Many ethical questions are raised by contemporary tourism practices.

étude de faisabilité
feasibility study
A feasibility study on the implementation of a solar village was conducted.

faisable / réalisable
feasible / workable
A workable project.

s'évader
to escape / to get away from-it-all

Concern about the environment has spurred a growing number of tourists to seek alternatives to polluted beaches and mobbed capitals when they get away from-it-all.

besoin d'évasion
escapism

évaluation
assessment / evaluation
A preliminary assessment was made of the needs and problems in the region.

évaluer
to assess / to evaluate
The Center on Ecotourism and Sustainable Development's mission is to design, monitor, evaluate and improve ecotourism and sustainable tourism practices and principles.

évaluer le coût / calculer le coût
to cost out / to evaluate the cost / to determine the cost
They have to cost out a major construction project.

évaluation du coût / estimation du coût
costing

faune
wildlife
Tourists should avoid disturbing wildlife. They should be instructed on local wildlife behaviour and make sure they view it from an appropriate distance.
Tour operators should brief all clients and staff on the dangers of wildlife encounters.

financement
financing / funding

co-financement
co-financing / co-funding

financer
to finance / to fund
They were supposed to be funding environmentally sustainable projects across the Amazon.

flore
flora
To respect wildlife, flora and habitat.

flux touristiques
tourist flow
What are the implications of global climate change for tourist flows and seasonality?

It is necessary to prevent the gradual environmental degradation as a result of increased tourist flows.
International tourist flows should be analysed to estimate energy use associated with air travel.

maîtrise des flux touristiques
tourist flow management / visitor flow management

maîtriser les flux touristiques / les flux de visiteurs
to control tourist flows / to manage tourist flows

réglementer les flux touristiques
to regulate tourist flows
With alarm bells ringing over the melting of glaciers in the Himalayas, the government has decided to regulate tourist flows to the protected areas of Gangotri National Park.

folklore
folklore
Folklore: traditional knowledge handed down from generation to generation.

folklorique
folk

foule
crowd / mob (péj) / throng
Situated snugly among the Leeward Islands in the West Indies, unaffected by throngs of noisy tourists, these islands offer visitors a mix of Old World Charm and magnificent scenery.

bondé
crowded / packed / mobbed / thronged

loin de la foule bruyante
"far from the madding crowd"
Top of the wish list for eco-travellers are small islands, fringed with picture-postcard beaches and definitively far from the madding crowd!

gaspillage
waste
Tourists should use resources sustainably, reduce waste and overconsumption.

gaspiller
to waste

harceler les animaux
to harass animals

hors des sentiers battus
off the beaten track

s'aventurer hors des sentiers battus
to stray off the beaten track

hygiène
sanitation
"Water is life, sanitation is dignity."

identité
identity

identité nationale
national identity

impact / effet
impact
positive impacts ≠ negative impacts

minimiser les effets négatifs du tourisme
to minimize the negative impacts of tourism
With international tourism forecast to nearly triple in volume over the next 20 years, members of the World Tourism Organization believe that the Global Code of Ethics for Tourism is needed to help minimize the negative impacts of tourism on the environment and on cultural heritage while maximizing the benefits for residents of tourism destinations.

inexploré
unexplored / unchartered

intégrité
integrity

interdire
to ban / to prohibit / to forbid
Ivory trade should be banned.

langue
language

maîtriser une langue
to have a good command of a language
He has a good command of German.

limiter
to limit

limiter la taille d'un groupe
to limit the size of a group

limiter le développement touristique
to limit tourism development

limiter l'utilisation de
to cut back on the use of
We should cut back on the use of air-conditioning.

à long terme
over the long-term / in the long run
Sustainable development is viable over the long term because it results in a net benefit for the social, economic, natural and cultural environments of the area in which it takes place.

marchandage
bargaining / haggling

marchander
to bargain (for) / to haggle (for)
Bargaining for goods should always reflect an understanding of a fair wage.

menacer
to endanger / to threaten

menacé
endangered / threatened
Global warming has led to a new travel boom as holidaymakers embrace what tour operators are calling doomsday tourism – the urge to see some of the world's most endangered sites before they disappear for ever.
Many people are picking a holiday destination because it is threatened by environmental circumstances.

mettre un frein à
to curb / to put a rein on
Mineral exploitation needs to be curbed.

mettre en œuvre (un projet / une stratégie / une politique)
to implement (a project / a strategy / a policy)
It should be a priority for local authorities to formulate and implement proper cultural tourism policy in partnership with the private sector, and with the participation of citizens.

mise en œuvre
implementation
The implementation of wise policies for sustainable urban tourism that is respectful of heritage and local communities is recommended.

microcrédit
microcredit
The award of the Nobel Peace Prize to Bangladeshi economist Professor Muhammad Yunus has focused the attention of the world on microcredit. Microcredits are very small loans made to the rural poor in developing countries who normally do not qualify for traditional banking credit.

à la mode / en vogue
fashionable / trendy / catching on
Ecotourism is catching on!

mode de vie / manière de vivre
way of life
To discover unique ways of life.

mondialisation
globalisation

nature
nature
Across Europe, vacationers are rediscovering the joys of nature.

nature sauvage
wilderness
Popular parks from Acadia (Maine) to Yosemite (California) are jammed with visitors. The overcrowding is spreading raising environmental concern and threatening the "wilderness experience".

néfaste
harmful
A harmful project.

niveau de vie
standard of living / living standard
Tourism generates jobs and improves the standard of living of local communities.

observer
to watch

observation
watching
Animal watching is very popular.

observation des baleines
whale-watching
This park's grandeur owes much to its varied seashore, popular for strolling, beachcombing and whale-watching.

observation des oiseaux
bird-watching
Point Reyes Bird Observatory is one of the best places for bird-watching.

Organisation non-gouvernementale (ONG)
Non-governmental organisation (NGO)

parc national
national park
National parks are often major tourist attractions located in remote and marginalised rural areas.
Yosemite is America's first federal mandated park and the model upon which the American national park system was based.
Dartmoor is a national park, which means that it belongs to the nation as a heritage.

partenariat
partnership

partenariat public-privé
public-private partnership
Theres is a need for effective public-private partnerships to ensure the sustainable management of World Heritage Sites.

en partenariat avec / en association avec
in partnership with
To promote sustainable tourism in partnership with the private sector, NGOs, civil society organisations and government.

partenaire / partie prenante
stakeholder
It is the responsibility of all stakeholders in tourism to achieve more sustainable forms of tourism.

patrimoine
heritage
The protection of the heritage, and its presentation and transmission to future generations, are therefore ethical imperatives, inseparable from respect for the dignity of the human person and the "desire to live together" on the part of people and groups with different cultural identities.

patrimoine culturel
cultural heritage
The preservation and promotion of our cultural heritage is an ethical imperative.

patrimoine historique
historic heritage
Many countries have adopted regulations to protect their historic heritage.

patrimoine mondial de l'humanité
the World Heritage List
The 1972 Convention identifies and protects the sites on the World Heritage List that are considered to be of "outstanding universal value" and sets an example for safeguarding the thousands of sites around the world which are no less deserving of our respect.

être inscrit au patrimoine mondial de l'humanité
to be on the World Heritage List / to be inscribed on the World Heritage List
Of the 721 sites inscribed to date on the World Heritage List, 31 are in danger, threatened by a variety of forces ranging from poverty, war or environmental deterioration in particular to inadequate management or unsustainable tourism in general.

pêche
fishing

pêche à la ligne
angling

pêche à la mouche
fly fishing
The three most common methods of fly fishing for Irish river trout are wet fly, dry fly and nymph fishing.

pêcher
to angle / to fish
Trout fishing is fishing for sport, the enjoyment being in the challenge.

pêcheur
angler (ligne) / fisherman / fly-angler (mouche)
The icy, spring-fed waters of Hat Creek and Fall River present a challenge even to experienced anglers.

attirail de pêche / matériel de pêche
fishing tackle / fishing gear

parcours de pêche / parcours réservé
fishery
It is fundamental to the survival of fisheries that they be managed and used by anglers in a sustainable manner.

permis de pêche
fishing permit / licence
Fishing tackle shops can be excellent centres for angling information and will usually supply fishing permits for local waters.

saison de pêche
angling season

pénurie / manque
shortage / lack (of)
Do you realize there's a water shortage?

manquer de
to lack something / to be short of
to lack resources / infrastructure / facilities

photographier
to take photos

se faire photographier / se faire prendre en photo
to be photographed
Travellers should be aware of people's sensitivity to being photographed. They should always ask first.

préservation
conservation
Sustainable development requires the conservation of plant and animal species.

préserver
to conserve
Ecotourism is a form of responsible travel to natural areas in order to conserve the environment.

prise de conscience
awareness / consciousness
To favour tourist awareness.
There is a need to improve awareness and exchange of knowledge between those responsible for and affected by tourism and nature conservation.

prise de conscience collective
public awareness
Public awareness should be heightened.

priorité
priority
What's the top priority?
The safety and security of visitors is an absolute priority.

projet
project
Our projects range from conservation, ecotourism and teaching to humanitarian aid.

projet pilote
pilot project

promouvoir
to foster / to promote
As a non-governmental organization, The International Ecotourism Society is unique in its efforts to provide guidelines and standards, training, technical assistance, research and publications to foster sound ecotourism development.

protégé
protected

It is simply not acceptable that beaches once protected for turtles are now the domain of sunbathers, swimmers and ice cream vendors.

protéger
to protect
The mission of the Rainforest Alliance is to protect ecosystems and the people and wildlife that live within them by implementing better business practices for biodiversity conservation and sustainability.

rare / peu abondant
scarce
In many coastal destinations, geared for conventional beach tourism, the peak seasons coincide with dry periods when water resources might be scarce.

reboisement
reforestation / reafforestation
Conservationists in Rwanda have launched a reforestation project that aims to create a forest corridor to link an isolated group of chimpanzees to larger areas of habitat in Nyungwe National Park.

réduction de la pauvreté
poverty alleviation / poverty reduction
Ecotourism is a tool for poverty alleviation and biodiversity conservation.

réduire la pauvreté
to alleviate poverty / to reduce poverty
This report contradicts the widely-held view that tourism helps to alleviate poverty.

régions sauvages
wilds

renforcement des capacités
capacity-building
Capacity building is an ongoing process through which individuals, groups, organizations and societies enhance their ability to identify and meet development challenges.

répartition
distribution
The unfair distribution of resources.

répartir
to distribute / to share out

réserve d'animaux sauvages
wildlife reservation / wildlife park

réserve de chasse
game reserve

réserve naturelle
nature reserve / wildlife sanctuary
South Africa is proud of its rich natural heritage, which is being diligently protected in the many nature reserves and national parks.

respect
respect
Responsible tourism engenders respect between tourists and hosts, and builds local pride and confidence.
Respect for the diversity of religious, philosophical and moral beliefs is the foundation of responsible tourism.

dans le respect de
with respect for
Activities should be conducted with respect for archeological and cultural heritage.

respecter
to respect
To respect diversity.

respectueux
respectful (of)
Tourists should be respectful of natural and cultural environments.

responsable
responsible
Travellers should limit the negative impacts of tourism on the natural and cultural environment through the responsible use of resources, effective waste management and minimizing of pollution.

de façon responsable / de manière responsable
responsibly
We are urging tourists to act responsibly when trekking in the Andes.

comportement responsable
responsible practices / responsible behaviour

investissement socialement responsable
socially responsible investment (SRI)

tourisme responsable
responsible tourism
Is responsible tourism possible?

touriste responsable / voyageur responsable
responsible tourist / responsible traveller

responsablité
responsability

ressources naturelles
natural resources / raw materials

retombées
fallout / consequences

retombées économiques
economic fallout

retombées financières
financial fallout

safari
safari
International travellers to Namibia come to engage in purely leisure activities such as safaris and guided tours.

safari photo
photographic safari

faire un safari
to go on a safari
They have been going on safaris in South Africa for over twenty years.

organiser un safari
to run a safari
We are committed to running our safaris on the principles of responsible tourism.

sauvegarde
preservation
Responsible tourism makes positive contributions to the preservation of natural and cultural heritage, to the maintenance of the world's diversity.

sauvegarder
to safeguard
Sustainable tourism balances economic objectives with safeguarding and enhancing the ecological, cultural and social integrity of a country's heritage.
Jobs will be safeguarded with a potential to create many more for local people.

sensibiliser les touristes à
to awaken tourists to / to make tourists aware of / to raise tourists awareness of
Sustainable tourism can raise public awareness of the many goods and services provided by biological diversity and of the needs to respect traditional knowledge and practices.

solidarité
solidarity
The impacts of rural tourism range from community diversification, delineation of social boundaries to a shifting basis of community solidarity.

tourisme solidaire
solidarity tourism
For several years we have seen the emergence of solidarity tourism – a desire for alternative travel and humanitarian actions.
Volunteers have contributed to the success of solidarity tourism trips to African countries, generating income for deprived communities.

soutenir / défendre
to support / to back
We should support the legislation to ensure the protection of historic places and resources.
Awareness of the potential that tourism seems to hold has been growing and many developing countries have actively supported its development.

soutien
support
The support for self-help projects and employment of local guides contributes to the long-term sustainability of communities managing their own natural resources.

défenseur / partisan
supporter / backer
Supporters of tourism argue that Africa's culture, natural beauty and historic sites should be promoted more.

tendance
trend / tendency
The trend toward environmental enhancement and heritage protection is a great asset to the tourism industry.

tribu
tribe
The Ovambos settled in Namibia in the mid 1500s and early conflicts within the group segregated them into eight tribes.

vacances originales
holidays with a difference / unusual holidays

valeurs
values
Sustainable tourism is guided by the values of respect, integrity and empathy.

TOURISME URBAIN
Urban Tourism

abbatiale / abbaye
abbey / abbey church
Glastonbury and its ruined abbey are steeped in legend.
The abbey church was built in the neo-gothic style between 1870 and 1938.

animé
bustling / lively
Blackpool is a lively crowded, jostling resort, busiest during summer when the Lancashire mills close down for their annual holidays.

antiquités
antiques

magasin d'antiquités
antiques shop

marché aux antiquités
antiques market
Portobello is one of London's most historic markets and the leading antiques market in the UK.

marché aux puces / puces
flea market
Portobello Road antiques and flea market in Notting Hill takes place every Saturday.

salon des antiquaires
antiques fair

brocante
junk shop

vide-grenier
car boot sale
Car boot sales are a favourite pastime in Britain at the weekends.

antiquaire
antiques dealer
Bermondsey Antiques Market is a favourite among early risers from the UK and antiques dealers in Europe seeking antiques at very competitive prices.

brocanteur
junk dealer

architecture
architecture
From 1640 to 1830 almost all English architecture was inspired by the legacy of classical Rome.
The variety of architecture to be seen in Britain from prehistoric monuments to the skyscrapers of modern London provides a record of the nation's history.

architectural
architectural

partimoine architectural
architectural heritage
It is the castles, churches, cathedrals and country houses of Britain that represent the architectural heritage of the country and attract tourists.
English Heritage restores, conserves and maintains over 350 properties representing the wide range of England's architectural heritage.

architecte
architect
John Nash planned the rows of buildings that now form part of the outer circle of Regent's Park and line Park Square and Park Crescent.

art
art

artistique
artistic

capital artistique
artistic wealth / artistic resources

atout
asset / draw / drawing card
Taiwan's biggest tourist draw is the National Palace Museum in Tapei which contains over 600 000 Chinese artifacts.
Blackpool's promenade is its chief drawing card.

attrait
lure
Gujarat has many tempting lures: a festival of kites, a hilltop crowded with temples, sandy beaches…

autobus (urbain), autobus (inter-urbain)
bus / coach

arrêt d'autobus
bus stop

arrêt facultatif
request bus stop

bus panoramique
open-top bus

The best way to see a new city is from the top deck of an open-top bus.

bus à impériale
double-decker bus / Routemaster (London)

The legendary red double-decker buses that ply London streets offer the best value tour.

The Routemaster, with its hop-on, hop-off platform and a conductor, began to replace London's electric trolleybuses in 1956.

basilique
basilica

berceau (civilisation)
cradle

The cathedral of Canterbury is the Mother Church of Anglican Christendom, the cradle of English Christianity.

bidonville
shanty town

bibliothèque
library

This library shelves some 1.5 million books.

boîte aux lettres
mail box (US) / letter box / pillar box

bourg, bourgade
marketown

In the early 19th century Old Swindon was a typical hilltop market town of some 1,700 inhabitants.

bureau de location (théâtre, spectacles)
box office / ticket booth / ticket office

Tickets are available for most London fringe theatres from the Fringe Box Office in St Martin's Lane.

cabine téléphonique
phone booth / pay station (US) / public phone

capitale
capital / capital city

Sacramento, California's capital, brims with pioneer history and gold-rush allure.

carnaval
carnival

The Notting Hill Carnival is a street procession and festival which takes place in Notting Hill during the long bank holiday weekend at the end of August. It is organised by the Caribbean community in London. It is one of the largest street celebrations in Europe, and has been taking place annually for about 40 years.

cathédrale
cathedral

Canterbury cathedral is a treasure house of architectural skills from Norman times onwards and contains a magnificent collection of stained glass. Southwark Cathedral is surrounded by warehouses, a produce market and some interesting new architecture.

cloître
cloister

crypte
crypt

vitrail
stained-glass window

centre omnisports
sports centre

centre commercial
shopping centre / shopping mall (US)

centre ville
inner city centre / city centre / downtown (US)

Unlike many big cities, San Francisco still has its government, financial and major retail centres located downtown. Walking is a good way to take a look at downtown San Diego's large entertainment complexes, small museums and shopping opportunities.

chapelle
chapel

château
castle

Leeds castle was home to six of England's queens. One of its famous residents was King Henry VIII.

chiner
to poke about for antiques
Cape Cod is a great place to poke about for antiques.

cimetière
cemetery / graveyard
Jim Morrison is buried at Père Lachaise cemetery in Paris, where his grave has become a shrine for successive generations of fans.

comédie musicale
musical
Don't miss "Me and My Girl" – a musical sparkling with energy and zany humour!

dater (de)
to date back (to) / to date (from)
Powis Castle – a red limestone castle near Welshpool dates from the late 13th century.

déplacer (se) (dans une ville, un pays)
to get around / to get round
London's Underground Railway or "Tube" is the easiest and quickest way of getting round London.

droit d'entrée (exposition, musée, parc à thème...)
admission charge / entrance fee
One admission charge covers all activities.

> **faire payer l'entrée (de)**
> to charge admission (to)

> **entrée gratuite**
> admission free

église
church
Thatched cottages nestle in the shadow of the 15th century church, perched on a hill above the village.

époque
era / age
The Victorian age / The Victorian era.
The architecture in the Victorian age was characterized by the recreation of styles from the past, the use of coloured brick as decoration and by the introduction of new methods of construction using iron, steel and glass.

> **d'époque**
> period
> *South of Regent's Park, many streets offer long vistas of period buildings. Harley St, Wimpole St and Wigmore St are three of interest.*

espaces verts
green areas / open spaces

exposition (art)
exhibition
The Royal Academy stages its summer exhibition from May to August and mounts a number of other exhibitions throughout the year.

> **exposition temporaire**
> temporary exhibition

> **exposition universelle**
> World Fair

festival
festival
Over 180 artists from throughout the country display their works at Sausalito's annual Art Festival. Cincinnati is a year-round haven for cultural events, festivals and music.

> **festival de Cannes**
> Cannes Film Festival

> **festival lyrique**
> opera festival

concerts en plein air
open-air concerts

flâner
to stroll
They strolled by the river.
Experience Vizcaya – Miami's magnificent palace – and stroll through picturesque gardens enhanced by sculptured fountains and marble statuary!

floralies
flower show / horticultural exhibition
Holland's Floriade is the greatest flower show on earth!
Don't miss Floriade 1992, the World Horticultural Exhibition! It's a unique show of flowers, bulbs, plants, trees...

fontaine
fountain
The Trevi Fountain – a baroque landmark dating from the18th century – was popularised by films such as Federico Fellini's La Dolce Vita.

galerie d'art
art gallery
A unique collection of contemporary paintings, serigraphs and lithographs are for sale in this art gallery.

galerie marchande
shopping arcade

gothique
gothic
The pointed arch of the windows is characteristic of the whole gothic period and distinguishes it from the romanesque style of the round arches.

grands magasins
department stores
Harrods is one of the biggest and best-known department stores in London and attracts customers from all over the world.

gratte-ciel
skyscraper

guide touristique
guide book / touring guide / tour book (US)

habitant
dweller / inhabitant
In Little Venice, London, the houses, pubs and restaurants reflect the literary and artistic tastes and occupations of the inhabitants.

horaires d'ouverture / heures d'ouverture
business hours / opening times
The British Museum is open daily from 10am to 5.30 pm but some galleries may be subject to limited opening times.

hôpital
hospital

hôtel de ville
city hall / town hall

jardin public
park / public gardens
It is the parks, more than any other feature, which make London unique among the world's great capitals.

jardin botanique
botanical gardens
Athens, north-east of Atlanta, is home to the State Botanical Gardens of Georgia. Set in a forest along a scenic river, the garden provides a perfect environment to collect, display and study the native plant life.

The luxuriant botanical gardens extend over 75 acres with wide paths and lawns shaded by tropical trees.

jardin paysagé
landscaped gardens

jardin tropical
tropical gardens
Miami's Parrot Jungle is a unique tropical gardens where exotic flowering trees and plants are complemented by the world's most beautiful birds.

jardins suspendus
hanging gardens / terraced gardens

lèche-vitrine
browsing / window-shopping

> #### faire du lèche-vitrine
> to browse / to window-shop
> *They window-shopped in Regent Street.*

lieux d'intérêt touristique
places of interest / places to see
Cambridge's places of interest include the Colleges, the Folk Museum and Sedgwick Museum of Geology.

avoir lieu
to be held (at, in) / to take place (at, in)
Annual regattas are held at Burry Port in August.

ligne (d'horizon, des toits…)
skyline
The tallest structure on the San Francisco skyline is the Trans America Pyramid.
With a new skyline of thrilling colours and futuristic designs, Miami's downtown area has become an international business mecca.

maison à colombages
half-timbered house
Houses in Grope Lane are typical of the town's numerous half-timbered houses dating back to the Elizabethan era.

maison blanchie à la chaux
whitewashed house
Lining the street are whitewashed 18th century houses decked with bright fuchsias and hydrangeas which seem to tumble down to the tiny harbour.

marché
market
When the produce markets left the area, Covent Garden's old buildings were saved and now form

a thriving fashionable market for crafts, presents, souvenirs and clothes.
London's markets are as various as they are colourful and fascinating. Petticoat Lane Market – formerly a place where the local poor would buy old clothes and cast-offs of the rich – now attracts many tourists.

marché au poisson
fish market
The fish market is a hive of activity in the early morning.

métropole
metropolis
Atlanta is an exploding metropolis of some 2 million people.

monument
monument
Westminster Abbey displays over 1,000 monuments and memorials to people notable in all aspects of British history.

monument classé
historic monument / listed monument / listed building
Buildings that are historically or architecturally important are recorded by the government as listed buildings and are subject to conservation laws.

mosquée
mosque

mur d'enceinte
surrounding wall / outer wall

musée
museum
The Jersey museum is housed in an old merchant's house and an adjoining 18th century warehouse.
Bath is the home of a wealth of museums.

musée d'art moderne
modern art museum

musée d'histoire naturelle
natural history museum

musée de cire
wax museum

musée des beaux arts
fine arts museum

musée des sciences
science museum

faire les musées
to visit museums

nef
nave
The austere nave-very tall, narrow and of white stone-is by Giles Gilbert Scott.

office de tourisme
Tourist Board / Tourism Office, Convention and Visitors Bureau
The London Tourist Board's main information centre is at Victoria Station. It will arrange hotel, theatre and tour bookings.

opéra (bâtiment)
opera house
Sydney's opera house is world-famous.

palais
palace
Kensington Palace

panneau
sign

panorama, point de vue
vista
With the glinting gold Victoria Memorial at one end and the bulk of Admiralty Arch at the other, the Mall is in high summer one of the best vistas London can offer.
From the hilltops on either side there are views far across the Camel River.
The views are spectacular.

paysage urbain
townscape / cityscape / urban landscape

pèlerinage
pilgrimage

lieu de pèlerinage
place of pilgrimage / pilgrimage site
The Basilica of St Madeleine was one of Europe's most important pilgrimage sites with tens of thousands pilgrims flocking there to pay homage to the reputed remains of Mary Magdalene.

faire un pèlerinage
to go on a pilgrimage / to make a pilgrimage
She made an annual pilgrimage to Benares.

pèlerin
pilgrim
Pilgrims were on their way to Mecca.

pelouse
lawn / grass

pelouse interdite
keep off the grass

(se) perdre
to get lost / to lose one's way
They got lost in the maze of narrow streets.

piéton
pedestrian

passage pour piétons
pedestrian crossing / zebra crossing

zone piétonne
pedestrian zone / pedestrian area
The city of York has one of the largest pedestrian zones in the UK.

rue piétonne
pedestrian street / foostreets
Footstreet create a safer and more attractive city centre for residents, shoppers and visitors.

pittoresque
picturesque / quaint
Woburn Walk is a quaint lane of bow-fronted well-preserved shops-everybody's idea of Dickens' London.

place
square
London's squares came into being in the 1630s, when Inigo Jones laid out Covent Garden.

plan de ville
city map

pont
bridge
Hamburg boasts 2,302 bridges-more than Venice and Amsterdam combined.

posséder (être fier de..., se vanter de...)
to boast
Bruges boasts picturesque canals.

poste
post office

poster (lettre)
to mail (a letter, a postcard...) / to post

quartier
area / district / neighborhood (US)

quartier commerçant
shopping district

quartiers pauvres
slums

quartier résidentiel
residential area / uptown (US)

remparts
ramparts / walls

rue
street

impasse
blind alley / dead-end street

rue à sens unique
one-way street

rue principale
high street / main street

ruelle
alley / backstreet

rues pavées
cobbled streets

un lacis de ruelles
a maze of backstreets / a maze of twisting backstreets

style gothique / moyenâgeux / roman / renaissance / contemporain
gothic / medieval / romanesque / renaissance / contemporary style

style gothique perpendiculaire anglais
perpendicular style

surpeuplé
cramped / overcrowded

syndicat d'initiative
tourist information centre / visitor information center (US)

théâtre
theatre / theater (US)
The RSC, the National Theatre and the summer open-air theatres in Holland Park and Regent's Park perform Shakespeare's work regularly.

théâtre en plein air / représentations en plein air
open-air theatre / open-air performances

pièce de théatre
play

sanctuaire
sanctuary / henge monument
Henge monuments which are unique to Britain consisted of a bank and ditch, nearly always circular, which enclosed a sacred area sometimes containing a ring of ritual pits or rings of standing stones.

toit
roof

toit en ardoise
slate roof
A village of reddish stone houses with slate roofs.

tramway
cablecar / streetcar / tramway

université
college / university
Trinity College, Dublin, is well worth a visit!

urbain
urban

zone urbaine
urban zone
Toulouse is one of the fastest growing urban zones in France thanks to Airbus and the aerospace industry.

urbanisme
town-planning / urban planning
The unparalleled harmony and elegance of Bath's 18th century architecture and urban planning combined with its ancient past and its lively present makes the city popular with visitors throughout the year.

urbaniste
town-planner, urban planner

équipement urbain
town facilities

réaménagement des zones urbaines
urban renewal

village
village

village carte postale
picture postcard village

ville
city / town
Welcome to Miami, a vibrant metropolis fast becoming the city of the future!
Because of its architectural design the city is best seen on foot.

périphérie
city outskirts

ville fantôme
ghost town
Bodie is one of the best preserved mining ghost towns in America.

ville frontalière
border town

ville natale
birthplace
Stratford-upon-Avon was Shakespeare's birthplace.

ville sainte
holy city

visite (d'une ville)
sightseeing tour / tour
Tours start at 9 am and leave every 30 minutes from convenient locations.

visite guidée
guided tour / escorted tour

visite à pied
walking tour
Enjoy a walking tour taking you back through Mercado's legendary past!

zoo
zoological gardens / zoo
London Zoo celebrates 180 years of being open, showing the animals of the world in the centre of London. It is open every day of the year except Christmas Day.

TRANSPORT
Transport, transportation (US)

--- **1** ---
TRANSPORT AÉRIEN
Air transport

accident d'avion
plane crash
No one is believed to have survived the crash of Gol Airlines Flight 1907 in Brazil's Amazon region.

s'écraser
to crash
An Egyptian charter plane has crashed into the Red Sea, killing all 148 passengers and crew on board.

catastrophe aérienne
air disaster

aérien
air

avoir de mal de l'air
to be airsick

aérodrome
airfield

aérogare
terminal
Stansted's terminal is being enlarged to cope with the overspill from Heathrow, Gatwick and Luton. Don Muang Airport provides passengers with all the facilities you would expect at a modern international terminal.

aéroport
airport
Gatwick Airport is a mere 30 minutes from Victoria Station.

hall (aéroport)
terminal / air terminal / airport terminal
Airport terminals will become ever more com-mercial. From glossy shopping malls to virtual-reality games, retail is increasingly visible.

hall d'arrivée
arrival terminal

hall de départ
departure terminal

taxe d'aéroport / taxe aéroportuaire
airport tax

affréter (un avion)
to charter (a plane)
They chartered a plane to Sydney.

altitude de croisière
cruising altitude
When the engines slow as the plane reaches a cruising altitude, the decibel level drops to 110.

annuler (une réservation, un vol)
to cancel

annulation
cancellation

atterrir
to land / to touch down
We have just landed at Gatwick Airport.

atterrissage
landing

atterrissage forcé
ditching / emergency landing / forced landing

faire un atterrissage forcé
to ditch

avion
aircraft (pl.: aircraft) / airplane / plane

avion sanitaire
flying ambulance

peur en avion / stress aéronautique
fear of flying
Often unacknowledged or neglected, the fear of flying can be a severe handicap in today's world.

avion-cargo
freighter

avion charter
charter plane

avion gros porteur
jumbo jet

prendre l'avion
to take the plane

voyager en avion
to fly / to travel by plane
In three separate travel surveys 89% of business travellers said they prefer to fly long haul in a configuration without a middle seat.

avion + croisière / avion + train / avion + voiture
fly-cruise / fly-rail / fly-drive

bagages
baggage (US) / luggage (sg.: a piece of luggage)

bagage à main
carry-on luggage / hand luggage / carry-on
Airlines are considering redefining carry-ons. Check that the size of your hand luggage does not exceed the dimensions permitted on board.

limiter les bagages à main
to clamp down on carry-on bags
Airlines started clamping down on carry-on bags after flight crews raised concerns about bags spilling out of packed overhead bins.

coffre à bagages
overhead compartment / overhead locker / overhead bin (US)
They have increased the size and length of the overhead lockers on all their flights. This will create more space for hand luggage stowage.
Passengers are requested to stow their hand luggage in the overhead compartments.
May I ask you to stow your raincoat in the overhead compartment?

étiquetage des bagages
baggage tagging

soute à bagages
baggage hold

franchise (bagages)
free baggage allowance

baptême de l'air
first flight

(à) bord
aboard / on board
Most airlines now allow fliers to bring aboard diaper bags, camera bags, umbrellas, infant seats in addition to 2 carry-on bags.

bienvenue à bord
"welcome on board!"
Captain Smith and his crew are happy to welcome you aboard this Boeing 767 to Atlanta.

ventes à bord
in-flight shopping

billet d'avion / titre de transport aérien
air ticket / plane ticket

émettre un billet d'avion / un titre de transport
to issue a plane ticket
The following taxes are charged on all tickets issued in the French department of Reunion Island.

billet électronique
e-ticket

aller simple /aller retour
one-way ticket, single ticket / return ticket / round-trip ticket (US)

boîte noire
black box / flight recorder

boutique hors-taxe
duty-free shops / tax-free airport shop
Duty-free shops are a handy place to spend a little time and money on a dull journey.
For the operators of tax-free airport shops, bored travellers mean booming turnovers.

achats hors-taxe / ventes hors-taxe
duty-free purchases / duty-free sales
The single market has put an end to duty-free purchases within the European Union.

carburant
fuel

sur-taxe carburant
fuel surcharge
The largest American carriers have increased fuel surcharges by $20 for round-trip tickets.

chef de cabine
purser
Pursers on each flight ensure that your travel needs are met.

classe affaires
business class

classe économique
economy class

In general terms, on short flights there is not a lot of difference between economy and business classes. This contrasts with transatlantic and Far Eastern long-haul flights.

compagnie aérienne
airline

European airlines are beginning to introduce Frequent Flier Programs (FFPs), more specifically targeted toward business travellers than the general catch-all approach of those in North America.

companies aériennes nationales
national flag carriers

complet
booked up / fully booked

correspondance
connection / connecting flight

correspondance entre deux lignes aériennes
interline connection

passagers en correspondance
connecting passengers

Flight connection desks offer check-in and ticketing facilities for connecting passengers.

créneau horaire
slot

créneau d'atterrissage
landing slot

créneau de décollage
take-off slot

Bigger carriers tend to have more weight to throw around, locking up landing slots at hubs and offering incentives to travel agents for preferential bookings.

décalage horaire
jet-lag

souffrir du décalage horaire
to be jet-lagged

décoller
to take off

We shall take off shortly.

décollage
taking-off

débarquer
to deplane / to disembark / to get off the plane

carte de débarquement
landing card

déréglementation
deregulation

Deregulation may mean lower air fares, so more passengers and more overcrowding in the sky.

déréglementer
to deregulate

In the two decades since the American industry was deregulated, it has seen wild expansion with more than 100 new carriers launched in the 1980s, followed by equally manic consolidation with more than 100 failures and takeovers in the 1990s.

dérouter (un avion)
to divert / to re-route (a plane)

desservir
to link / to serve

We now serve nine major European cities. 101 US cities are served by Air France.

destination
destination

départ à destination de...
departure to...

économies d'échelle
economies of scale

United wants US air to broaden its services nationally along with increasing its economies of scale.

écran radar
radar screen

The plane disappeared from radar screens shortly after take-off.

embarquer
to board (a plane) / to embark / to get on (a plane)

Economy class passengers are requested to board now.

embarquement
boarding

Boarding will take place according to the seat numbers shown on the boarding cards.

absence à l'embarquement
no show

passagers no show / passagers qui ne se présentent pas sur le vol pour lequel ils ont une réservation
no show passengers

ne pas se présenter à l'embarquement
not to show up
An average 10 to 15% of passengers do not show up for the flight.

carte d'embarquement
boarding card / boarding pass

porte d'embarquement
boarding gate
Immediate boarding! Passengers for this flight should proceed to Gate 8.

pré-embarquer
to pre-board
Such passengers as unaccompanied minors (UMs) are normally pre-boarded.

pré-embarquement
pre-boarding

encombrement (aérien)
air congestion / backup (US)
Big improvements will have to be made to ease air congestion over Britain.

le ciel est encombré
the skies are busy / the skies are crowded

enregistrer (bagages)
to check in

enregistrement
check-in
*Advanced check-in / separate check-in…
An increasing number of airlines are creating downtown check-in facilities.*

enregistrement des bagages
baggage check-in / luggage check-in

bagages enregistrés jusqu'à la destination finale
through checked baggage
Through-checked baggage need not be reclaimed.

aire d'enregistrement des passagers
check-in area

comptoir d'enregistrement
check-in counter / check-in desk

équipage / personnel navigant
crew
The cabin crew have a number of duties to perform both before the passengers board and during boarding.

membres d'équipage
crew members

escale
layover (US) / stopover

faire escale (à)
to lay over (at) (US) / to stop over (at)
Passengers have to stop over at Atlanta and change plane to San Francisco.

espace aérien
air space
Europe has unnecessarily fragmented its air space.

espace pour les jambes
legroom / legspace

fiabilité, sérieux
reliability
It's surely one of the best airlines in terms of reliability and service!

fiable
reliable

flotte aérienne
fleet
We operate one of the largest and most modern fleets of any airline in the world.

moderniser la flotte aérienne
to relift the fleet / to upgrade the fleet
*Alitalia Express is upgrading its fleet.
The fleet will be relifted over the next 9 months.*

franchisage
franchising

fuseau horaire
time-zone

fusion
merger
Whatever efficiencies there may be in mergers, they rarely result in savings for flyers.

fusionner
to merge

gagner des points ciel, accumuler des miles
to collect frequent-flyer air miles / to earn miles / to gain air credit
Every time you fly on an eligible fare with us, you'll earn miles. You can then exchange these for flights to over 600 destinations worldwide.

horaire
schedule
This airline offers you convenient schedules and immediate connections spanning four continents!

hôtesse (de l'air)
air-hostess / cabin attendant (C.A.) / flight attendant
Cabin attendants must ensure that passengers fasten their seatbelts.
Some flight attendants have complained about their noisy work environment.

hub, plate-forme de correspondances, de connexions
hub
Crossair offers a network that encompasses over a 100 destinations in over 30 countries through its hub at EuroAirport Basel.

interdire
to ban / to forbid / to prohibit
Airlines ban the oversized bags that some fliers bring aboard.

liaison (aérienne)
airlink / link
The decision made by TWA to discontinue several air links led to general protest.
The era of glasnost spurred both Pan Am and Aeroflot to search for a high-capacity airlink.

lignes intérieures
domestic airlines / feeder airlines

lignes régulières
scheduled airlines (ant.: non-scheduled airlines)
When charter flights developed, scheduled airlines introduced fare reductions, tourist, then economy class.

long courrier / moyen courrier
long haul / medium haul

masque à oxygène
oxygen mask
Should the cabin lose pressure, oxygen masks will drop from the overhead area.

mur du son
sound barrier
franchir le mur du son
to break the sound barrier

navette
shuttle / shuttle bus
You will be transferred to your hotel in our complimentary shuttle.

ouvrir (une ligne)
to open (an air route, a regular flight…) / to begin (a new route, scheduled flights…)
Pan Am and Aeroflot are two of the world's pioneering airlines, with traditions of opening new air routes and flying long distances.

paralyser
to cripple
Air traffic was crippled by the Gulf War.

parcours
route
There are two Airbus routes running directly to all terminals at Heathrow, picking up at 13 points throughout the main hotel areas of Central London.
Charles Lindbergh surveyed transpacific and transatlantic routes for Pan Am.

partage de code
code share / code sharing
The new code-sharing services provide for the coordination of all boarding operations, including check-in, boarding cards, baggage check and flight schedules.

partir
to depart / to leave
Today more than 600 Thai International flights depart Bangkok each week for 72 destinations in 36 countries across four continents.

pass aérien
air pass

passager
passenger / flyer / flier (US)
Since 1975, the number of air passengers in Europe has grown on average by nearly 6% a year far faster than governments or airlines predicted.

In the U.S.A., passenger numbers more than doubled in the decade after deregulation.

passager classe économique
coach-class flier / economy class passenger
Northwest Airlines has limited coach-class fliers to one carry-on bag plus a laptop, briefcase or purse.

passager première classe
first-class passenger
Some airlines offer noise-cancelling headphones to first-class passengers.

personnel navigant
flight attendants

piste (d'envol, d'atterrissage)
airstrip / runway

place / siège (avion)
seat
The seats to avoid on any airplane fall into three categories: non-reclining, middle and restroom adjacent.

place /siège côté hublot
window seat

place / siège côté couloir
aisle seat

place / siège du milieu
middle seat

attribuer /affecter une place
to assign a seat

attribution d'une place
seat assignment
Request a seat assignment when you book your flight.

report d'embarquement volontaire
voluntary bumping
Voluntary bumpings – where fliers voluntarily give up seats in exchange for incentives such as travel vouchers – have hit an all-time high.

ponctualité
ponctuality
Neither the staff nor passengers are happy with the airline's ponctuality record.

programme de fidélisation
frequent flyer programme
Club MilleMiglia, Alitalia's frequent Flyer programme was devised to offer passengers flying with Alitalia maximum benefits and services.

Passengers are credited with a number of miles equal to the distance flown.

quasi-collision
near-miss
Air traffic has increased to the extent of causing air congestion especially during the peak season and grim stories of near-misses are reported.

récupérer les bagages
to reclaim baggage / to reclaim luggage
Through-checked baggage doesn't need to be reclaimed until the final destination.

retrait des bagages
baggage reclaim
Baggage must be collected at baggage reclaim.

règlementation / règlement
regulations / rules
As part of our flight is over the water, international regulations require that we demonstrate the use of life-jackets.
No regulations have been introduced to prevent airlines from slashing prices.

règlement de propriété des compagnies aériennes
airline-ownership rules

retarder (un vol)
to delay (a flight)

retardé (de...)
delayed (by...) (ant.: on time)
Almost a quarter of all intra-European flights were delayed by more than 15 minutes last year.

retard
delay

rouler (avion)
to taxi
The aircraft leaves the ramp, taxies to the runway, lines up and takes off.

sécurité
safety / security
For your safety, please study the passenger safety information card when boarding the aircraft.

contrôle de sécurité
security check

sécurité des passagers
passenger safety
Unruly and disruptive passengers can endanger passenger safety through undisciplined and aggressive behaviour.

ceinture de sécurité
safety belt
The sign to keep seatbelts fastened has been turned off.

consignes de sécurité
safety instructions

normes de sécurité
safety standards

raisons de sécurité
safety reasons
For safety reasons, please do not put the following in your hand luggage: compressed gases, corrosives, explosives, solified and inflammable liquids and other substances or objects listed in the regulations attached to every plane ticket.

service clientèle
customer service
Passengers can receive information on the frequent flyer programme by calling the customer service.
A dedicated customer service operating Monday through Friday has been set up.

sol (au)
ground (on the)
SAS excels on the ground where it has started city centre check-ins.

   personnel au sol
   ground staff
   This airline boasts an efficient ground staff.

supprimer
to cancel (a flight) / to discontinue (an airlink)
This airline is going through dire financial straits; several airlinks will have to be discontinued.

surbooker / surréserver / pratiquer le surbooking
to overbook
Airlines routinely overbook seats because 10% to 15% of passengers, often business travellers with expensive and refundable tickets do not show up.

   surbooké / surréservé
   overbooked
   There has been a surge in overbooked seats.

   surbooking / surréservation
   overbooking
   Without overbooking ticket prices would have to be higher to compensate for the empty seats.

syndrome de la classe économique
economy class syndrome / deep vein trombosis (DVT)
DVT is believed to affect passengers who sit in cramped conditions for long hours without exercise.

tablette
tray table

   relever la tablette
   to put the tray table up
   Before take-off, put your seat in an upright position, your tray table up and fasten your seatbelt.

tarif aérien
air-fare

   tarif excursion
   APEX fare

   tarif négocié
   negotiated fare

   système de tarification différenciée
   yield management

   base tarifaire
   fare basis

   codification tarifaire
   fare coding

   disponibilité tarifaire
   fare availability

tour de contrôle
control tower
There was no distress call from the plane to the control tower.

trafic aérien
air-traffic
Investment in better air-traffic control equipment, together with a redesign of the routes used by aircrafts should free more airspace.

contrôleur aérien
air-traffic controler

trafic de passagers
passenger traffic
Thanks to the absence of a central concourse, passenger traffic flows smoothly without confusion or bottlenecks.

transfert
transfer

transport aérien
air transport

transporter (passagers)
to carry (passengers)
The Jumbo Jet can carry up to 500 passengers.
Many dangerous materials can be transported when packed according to cargo regulations.

transporteur aérien
carrier / air carrier
Foreign carriers should be allowed to compete for French domestic passengers to keep fares as low as possible.
US Air, the country's sixth largest carrier, specialises in shorter trips.

turbulences
turbulence (uncount)
Turbulence caused the plane to turn over.
A British Airways jumbo jet on its way from Australia to Singapore was so badly buffeted by turbulence that one man was thrown into the overhead lockers.

traverser une zone de turbulences
to experience air turbulence

trou d'air
clear air turbulence
Six people were mildly injured when a Boeing 777 hit a pocket of severe "clear air turbulence".

vitesse de croisière
cruising speed
Our cruising speed will be 570mph.

vol
flight
The use of cell phones on board in our flights is permitted only before the aircraft doors are closed.

vol court courrier
shorthaul flight

vol long courrier
longhaul flight

vol charter
charter flight

vol direct
non-stop flight

vol intérieur
domestic flight

vol régulier
scheduled flight, regular service

ventes de vols secs
"seat only" sales
Demand for "seat only" sales has increased significantly as experienced holidaymakers choose to travel independently.

instruments de vol
flying instruments

plan de vol
flight plan

simulateur de vol
flight simulator
They rely on flight simulators to accustom fliers to turbulence and noise.

en vol
in-flight (adj.)
In-flight entertainment
In-flight magazine
The consumer affairs phone number is published in the in-flight magazine.

zone fumeur / zone non-fumeur
smoking area / no-smoking area / non-smoking area
The smoking area is located at the rear of the aircraft.

détecteur de fumée
smoke detector

——— 2 ———
TRANSPORT FERROVIAIRE
Rail transport

billet
ticket

billet demi-tarif
half-fare ticket

prix du billet
fare

contrevenant
fare-dodger
Fare-dodgers will be prosecuted.

distributeur automatique
ticket machine

buffet de la gare
station buffet bar

bureau des objets trouvés
lost-property office / lost and found office (US)

carte (de train) (abonnement général)
railcard / pass / railway pass / railroad pass (US)

carte vermeil
senior citizen railcard

carte d'abonnement
season ticket / commuter pass / commuter ticket (US)

abonnement mensuel / trimestriel / annuel
one-month commuter pass, monthly ticket / three-month commuter pass / yearly ticket

chariot à bagages
luggage trolley

chemins de fer
railways / railroads (US)
During the 19th century, railroads spread across Europe and North America. They formed the first successful system of mass transportation.
From the first half of the 19th century, a dense network of railways was built in Britain.

chemins de fer britanniques / américains
British Rail / Amtrak

circuler (train)
to run / to operate
Trains to Gatwick Airport run every hour from Victoria Station.
Several trains operate year-round; others are geared for summer vacationers.

collision
collision
Three trains were involved in a collision during morning rush hour in south London.

entrer en collision
to collide (with)
Rail passengers are facing disruption after a train collided with a van which had been abandoned on tracks.

catastrophe ferroviaire
rail disaster

compartiment
compartment
He only travels in first-class compartments.

compartiment fumeur / compartiment non-fumeur
smoking compartment / non-smoking compartment

composter (un billet)
to date-stamp (a ticket)
Don't forget to date-stamp your ticket before getting on the train.

machine à composter
date-stamping machine

consigne (bagages)
left-luggage office / baggage-room (US) / locker storage

consigne automatique
luggage-lockers

contrôleur
ticket-collector
The ticket-collector clips (= punches) the tickets.

correspondance (train)
connection / connecting train
Is there a connecting train to Glasgow?

dérailler
to leave the metals / to run off the rails

descendre (du train)
to get off (the train)
Don't forget to get off at the next station!

desservir
to call (at)
The 10 o'clock train calls at every station between Chatham and London.

être à l'heure (train)
to run on time

gare
station / railway station / rail terminal
Brunel designed Paddington Station in the 19th century and the first regular omnibus service began.

gare routière
coach station / bus depot (US)

chef de gare
station master

aller chercher quelqu'un à la gare
to meet somebody at the station

mener quelqu'un à la gare
to see somebody to the station

guichet
ticket office
You can buy your ticket either at the ticket office or from a machine.

horaires / grille horaire
timetable / schedule (US)

indicateur horaire
railway schedule / railroad schedule (US)

kiosque
bookstall / newsstand (US)

liaison feroviaire
rail link
EU aid distribution, the advent of the single currency and improved rail links have pushed attention on to France's peripheral regions.
The Chunnel provides a direct rail link between Paris and London.
In Frankfurt, the new high-speed rail link to the city's airport should boost the hotel market.

lignes de banlieue
commuter lines / suburban lines

grandes lignes
inter-city lines

lignes secondaires
branch lines
Branch lines are being restored and offer rides through picturesque scenery and a visit to the railway museum.

ligne à grande vitesse
high speed line / high speed rail line
Eurostar has set a record on its inaugural journey from Paris to London via a new high-speed line in Britain.

manquer (un train / une correspondance)
to miss a train / to miss a connection

métro
undergroud / the Tube (London) / subway (US)
The Underground or Tube is the fastest and easiest way to get around Central London.

    station de métro
    underground station / tube station

monter (dans un train)
to board (a train) / to get on (a train) (ant.: to get off)

passionné de trains
train-spotter
Train-spotters visit stations and collect the numbers of the locomotives they see.

observation des trains
train-spotting
The hobby of train-spotting dates from the age of the steam train.

observer les trains (pour identifier les différents types de locomotives)
to go train-spotting

passerelle
footbridge

perturbation
disruption
France faces rail disruption in its worst ever transport strike, with only one-third of trains running.

    être perturbé
    to be disrupted
    Rail services were severely disrupted last week.

place (train)
seat

    place côté fenêtre / place côté couloir
    window seat / aisle seat

prendre le train (pour se rendre à son travail)
to commute
Many teachers commute on the high-speed train everyday.
Commuting to work can be a trial!

    usager (régulier, banlieusard)
    commuter

quai (train)
platform
On the platform an electronic board will remind you that the next train to Rochester is due at 11 a.m.

    abri (sur le quai)
    platform shelter

quitter la gare (train)
to depart from the station / to leave the station / to pull out of the station
I'm afraid you've missed the train to Brentwood! It has just pulled out of the station.

relier
to connect / to link
France's high-speed train network will be extended so as to link the Chunnel (Channel + Tunnel) with cities like Brussels.
Hong Kong's airport comes complete with a 35 km railway linking the airport to Hong Kong's Central District in 20 minutes.

relié (à)
connected (with) / linked (with)
All main line stations – that is the Intercity service to all parts of Britain – are connected with the Underground service.

relié par chemin de fer
linked by rail

réseau (ferroviaire)
(railway) network
A Britrail pass allows unlimited travelling on the entire British Rail network
In Europe, there is the Eurocity network linking about 200 towns and cities.

retardé
delayed / late
Is the train to Manchester delayed?

salle d'attente
waiting-room

signal d'alarme
alarm

tirer le signal d'alarme
to pull the alarm

supplément
excess fare

tunnel ferroviaire
rail tunnel
Lyons' transalpine connection is set to grow as the French and Italian governments look likely to approve studies for a 56 km rail tunnel under Mont Blanc.

train
train
Most trains have air-conditioned coaches with wide, double-glazed windows, and reclining seats if you're travelling first class.

eurostar
eurostar

train supplémentaire
extra train

train auto-couchettes
motorail
Day or night motorail takes the stress out of long distance driving.

train à crémaillère
cog-wheel train

train direct
fast train / through train

T.G.V.
bullet train / high-speed train
High speed train networks make intercity business travel much quicker and easier.

trains grandes lignes
intercity trains / long distance express trains

train panoramique
scenic railway

train supplémentaire
extra train

train touristique
tourist rail

funiculaire
cable-railway

omnibus
slow train

train + auto
rail-drive

train de marchandises
freight train

train à vapeur
steam train
The age of the steam train is viewed with nostalgia by many British people.

train + vélo
biking by train

voyager en train
to ride a train / to travel by train
When you ride a train, you can relax and avoid the hassles of traffic.
Ride the rails through the scenic and spectacular New River Gorge in West Virginia.
If riding the rails is your passion, northern California offers some nostalgic excursions and interesting museums.

voyage en train
train journey / train ride

wagon
carriage / car (US) / coach / railcar (US)
The Napa Valley Wine Train shuttles wine-lovers from vineyard to vineyard in vintage railcars.

wagon-lit
sleeping car / sleeper (US)

wagon restaurant
buffet car / dining car / restaurant car

wagon à deux étages (US)
double-decker car (US)

3
TRANSPORT FLUVIAL ET MARITIME
Water transport

accoster
to come alongside

aéroglisseur
hovercraft

amarrer
to tie up
The boat was tied up alongside a crumbling jetty.

ancre
anchor

être à l'ancre / jeter l'ancre / lever l'ancre
to lie at anchor / to cast anchor, to drop anchor / to weigh anchor
They cast anchor in a secluded harbour.

ancrage
anchorage
At the southernmost tip of Key Biscayne, anchorage is limited to three nights per month per vessel.

appareiller (bateau)
to get under way

bateau
boat / ship (fem.)

bateau à aubes
paddle-boat / paddle-wheel boat
In Augusta, visitors can stroll along the banks of the Savannah River or enjoy a moonlit cruise aboard a replica 19th century paddle-boat.

bateau de croisière
cruise liner / cruise ship
Our cruise ships offer all the amenities of a resort hotel.

bateau à vapeur
steamboat

bateau mouche
pleasure steamer

(à) bord
aboard / on board / shipboard
Aboard, all your needs are covered in your overall cruise cost with the exception of incidental items such as wine, cigarettes, laundry, shore excursions...
We offer you the best-informed and most convenient way of seeing the Galapagos islands, combining on-board lectures with in-situ excursions ashore to study the flora and the fauna.
The shipboard environment which we have created allows families to experience a bonding of sorts; they tell us that they leave the ship feeling closer as a family unit.

livre de bord
log-book

cabine
cabin

cabine intérieure / extérieure
inside cabin, cabin without a view / outside cabin, cabin with a view
The price per passenger ranges from £800 in a two-berth inside cabin to £1500 for a single-berth outside cabin.

cabine de luxe
stateroom
All our staterooms are handsomely appointed.

cap
cape
Magellan rounded Cape Horn and came north again up the coast of Chile.

mettre le cap (sur)
to head (for)

cargo
cargo-boat / freighter

chavirer / faire chavirer
to capsize

Two rowers rescued from the Indian ocean believe a whale probably capsized their tiny boat.

compagnie de navigation
shipping company

coque
hull

Two anglers have been airlifted to safety after spending up to 12 hours clinging to the upturned hull of their boat off the Pembrokeshire coast.

couchette (bateau)
berth

Accommodation is in spacious two-berth cabins with all the comfort you may require.

croisière
cruise

Why not try expedition cruises to exotic lands?

croisière sur un lac / sur une rivière
lake-cruise / river-cruise

croisière à thème
special-purpose cruise

Special-purpose cruises are getting more and more popular with those interested in architecture, archeology, wild life...

faire une croisière / partir en croisière
to cruise / to go on a cruise / to take a cruise

Cruising is by far the best way to see Alaska, because so much of its beauty lies near the shoreline.

à destination (de) / en partance (pour)
bound (for)

Step aboard a Love Boat bound for Alaska and enter a world unlike anything you have ever experienced before.

écluse
lock

éclusier
lock-keeper

ouvrir / fermer une écluse
to manoeuvre a lock / to open the gates / to lock the gates

ferry
ferry / ferry-boat

Ferries from Long Beach and San Pedro shuttle passengers to and from Avalon on an hourly basis.

embarquer
to board / to embark / to go on board

équipage
crew

Our yachts, taking a maximum of 12 persons are fully staffed with crew, steward and chef.

escale, port d'escale
port of call

Ports of call have been chosen for their fabulous and varied scenery, culture and fascinating places to explore.

hublot
porthole

itinéraire
itinerary

This newly refurbished ship recently began an exclusive itinerary to the Abacos Islands in the northern Bahamas, featuring visits to four separate islands.

loger
to accommodate

Increasing numbers of vacationers are opting for vessels accommodating fewer passengers and able to take them to quiet ports and secluded beaches.

maritime
seafaring

Great Britain has always been a seafaring nation.

naufrage
shipwreck

The crew perished in a shipwreck.

faire naufrage
to be shipwrecked

They were shipwrecked off the Bahamas.

navette
shuttle

effectuer la navette (bateau, véhicule...)
to shuttle

naviguer
to sail

For an unforgettable departure be on deck as you sail through San Francisco's legendary Golden Gate Bridge.

faire le tour du monde en bateau
to sail round the world

paquebot
liner

When you take a cruise on our luxury liner, you enter a world of pleasure and relaxation where comfort, wining and dining and entertainment are of the utmost importance.

passerelle (bateau)
gangway

péniche
barge

naviguer en péniche
to barge

Barging is both educational and pleasurable.

marinier
bargee / bargeman

phare
lighthouse

The lighthouse on South Stack, a rocky island off Holyhead Mountain, was built in 1809.

pont (bateau)
deck

sur le pont
on deck

Relax out on deck as your ship glides past forests in a thousand shades of green.

pont promenade
promenade deck / sun deck

jeux
deck-games / deck-sports

Deck-games range from volley-ball, and shuffleboard to skeet shooting and paddle tennis. You will need clothes and footwear suitable for deck-sports.

port
harbour / port

The lack of a political consensus among the european countries is preventing action for developing port infrastructures on the Atlantic and the Mediterranean seaboards.

port de plaisance
marina / yachting harbour

At the foot of the cliffs of Kemptown is the marina.

quai (bateau)
quay / wharf (pl.: wharves)

traversée (maritime)
crossing / sea-crossing / sailing

The Dublin Swift began operation from Holyhead to Dublin in June 1999 and offers a choice of four sailings a day.

première traversée / traversée inaugurale
maiden voyage

Built in 1960 by Metro Goldwyn Mayer, the Bounty has sailed over 70,000 miles including her maiden voyage to Tahiti for the filming of "Mutiny on the Bounty".

faire une bonne traversée / une mauvaise traversée
to have a smooth crossing / a rough crossing

sauver
to rescue

sauvetage
rescue

bouée de sauvetage
life-buoy

canot de sauvetage
life-boat

gilet de sauvetage
life-jacket, life-vest (US)

(à) terre
ashore / on-shore

Spend your time ashore discovering the special flavour of each port of call.

On-shore excursions are not included in the price we are quoting.

voies navigables
inland waterways

Holland is criss-crossed by a vast network of inland waterways.

4
TRANSPORT ROUTIER
Road transport

accident de voiture
car accident

aire de repos
rest area

aire de stationnement
parking area

amende
fine / ticket (US)

artère principale
main thoroughfare

autoroute
motorway (GB) / expressway (US) / freeway (US-no toll) / turnpike (US-toll)

bretelle de raccordement
access road

auto-stoppeur
hitch-hiker

faire de l'auto-stop
to hitch-hike
They intend to hitch-hike to Greece.

avenue
avenue / parkway (US)
Parkways are wide roads lined with trees or parkland. One of the earliest was the Bronx River Parkway constructed in 1925.

bande d'arrêt d'urgence
hard shoulder / berm (US)

barrage routier
roadblock

barrage de police
police roadblock

camping-car
motorhome / camper / recreational vehicle / van

caravane
caravan / trailer (US)

carrefour
road junction / crossroads

carte grise
car licence

carte routière
map / road-map
A road-map of Sicily.
Free maps and guides for visitors can be obtained from the London Tourist Board.

ceinture de sécurité
seat-belt
It is compulsory for the driver and front seat passengers to wear seat belts. Back seat belts must also be worn.

attacher (ceinture)
to fasten (seatbelt) / to buckle up (US)
"Buckle up! It's the law!"

circulation
traffic
Suburban sprawl has meant clogged traffic over ever greater commuting distances as residents move farther and farther from the urban cores in search of affordable homes.

code de la route
highway code / road regulations (US)

conduire
to drive
Driving in Ireland can be a bit of a challenge if you are not used to driving on the left.

conducteur
driver

conduite à gauche
left-hand drive

conduite à droite
right-hand drive

conduire à gauche
to drive on the left / to drive on the left-hand side
In Ireland people drive on the left hand side of the road and all Irish vehicles are right hand drive.

contrôle radar
speed check

couloir de bus
bus lane

co-voiturage
car-pooling / car-sharing

crever
to have a puncture / to have a flat tire (US)

> **crevaison**
> puncture

> **pneu crevé / à plat**
> punctured tyre / flat tire (US)

> **pneu dégonflé**
> deflated tyre

déviation
detour (US) / diversion

essence
gas (US) / petrol

> **station service**
> filling station (US) / gas station (US) / petrol station

> **le plein !**
> full tank!

> **faire le plein**
> to fill (a car) up

embouteillage
bottleneck / congestion / tailback / traffic-jam
The new four-lane highway from Albertville should put an end to the appalling bottlenecks that have plagued the area.

> **embouteillé**
> clogged / congested / jammed

emmener (quelqu'un en voiture)
to give (someone) a lift
Can you give me a lift to London?

feu (de circulation)
traffic lights
At the second set of traffic lights after the Park & Ride, turn left into Cricketers Lane.

fourrière
city car pound

> **mettre une voiture en fourrière**
> to impound a car / to tow away a car
> *Why was my car towed away?*

zone de mise en fourrière
tow-away zone

freiner
to brake

> **frein à main**
> handbrake

heures de pointe
peak hours / rush hours (ant.: slack hours)
Avoid taking the Tube at rush hours! All London stations are teeming with commuters.

impasse
blind-alley / cul-de-sac

kilométrage illimité
unlimited mileage

klaxonner
to honk one's horn / to hoot one's horn

limitation de vitesse
speed limit
Do not exceed the speed limit!
Highway speed limit is 55mph unless otherwise posted.

louer (véhicule)
to rent
Why not rent a convertible?

> **agence de location de voitures**
> car rental agency

> **conditions de location**
> rental terms

> **contrat de location**
> rental agreement

panneau de signalisation / panneau indicateur
road sign

parking
car park / parking-lot (US)

> **parc de stationnement (plusieurs niveaux)**
> multi-storey car park

> **se garer**
> to park
> *Can I park my car somewhere round here?*
> *You can't park here, you're on a double yellow line!*

se garer à l'extérieur des grandes agglomérations et emprunter les transports en commun
to park and ride

panne
breakdown

tomber en panne
to breakdown

péage
toll

barrière de péage
turnpike / tollgate

poste de péage
toll booth

route à péage
toll road / turnpike (US)

périphérique / bretelle de contournement
by-pass / ring road / underpass

permis de conduire
driving licence / driver's licence (US)

piste cyclable
cycle path / cycle track (US)
In Yosemite national park, free shuttle buses and paved cycle paths link all of the valley's camping, lodging and visitor centers, making it possible to get along just fine without a car.

plaque minéralogique
licence plate (US) / number plate / registration plate

poser un sabot
to clamp a vehicle / to clamp a car
If a clamped vehicle is not claimed within 24 hours, it will be towed away.

pose de sabot
clamping / wheel clamping

ralentir
to slow / to slow down

ralentissement
tailback
A 11 mile-tailback.

ralentisseur / gendarme couché
speed bump / sleeping policeman

réseau routier
road network

rond-point
roundabout

route
road
The oldest roads in Britain are the straight roads built by the Romans.

route départementale
B-road (GB) / minor road / rural highway / feeder road

route nationale
A-road (GB) / major road / highway (US) / interstate (US)

emprunter une route
to take a road
Take the first road on the left after the roundabout. Then it's straight on!

sortie d'autoroute
exit

système de guidage par ordinateur
GPS (Global Positionning Systems)
Car rental companies are trying their hands at technology, using new GPS to help lost travellers. GPS gives directions and tracks the progress of the vehicle.

stationnement
parking
Parking regulations are designed to make life more pleasant, to eliminate obstructions and reduce congestions, to improve road safety and to increase the availability of on-street parking spaces.

place de stationnement
parking space / parking slot / parking place

ticket de stationnement (à poser sur le pare-brise)
pay-and-display ticket
If the time allowed on a pay-and-display ticket has expired, your vehicle may be clamped or towed away.

taxi
cab / taxi / taxicab
They'll take a taxi back to the hotel.

héler un taxi
to wave down a taxi

station de taxis
taxi rank / taxi stand (US)
There's a taxi rank just outside the airport.

chauffeur de taxi
taxi driver

prendre un client en charge
to pick up a fare

course / prix de la course (taxi)
fare

course (prix forfaitaire)
flat fare

transports en commun
public transport / public transportation

travaux
road works
We were delayed by road works for one hour.

virage
bend / curve

> **virage en épingle à cheveux**
> hairpin bend

FORMALITÉS
Formalities

— 1 —
ASSURANCES
Insurance

---

annulation de voyage
trip cancellation
Travel insurance plans offer coverage for vacation and trip cancellation, travel interruptions, delays, emergency medical expenses and lost baggage.

annuler
to cancel
They cancelled their travel plans because of fear of terrorism.

assistance
assistance
All of our policies include access to a 24 hour emergency assistance helpline which can provide multi-lingual assistance, anywhere in the world.

assistance juridique
legal assistance
Many travellers are unaware of legal assistance available through most comprehensive travel insurance policies.

assistance médicale
medical assistance
You may fall ill and require medical assistance while travelling outside your country.

assurance
insurance (uncount)
Our insurance is focused on medical and emergency evacuation although it also covers other areas such as your baggage and cancellation costs. This holiday costs £1,589 plus insurance and airport taxes.

assurance annulation
cancellation insurance
We recommend you have cancellation insurance.

assurance automobile
car insurance

assurance individuelle
Personal Accident Insurance (PAI)

assurance multirisque
all-in insurance

assurance au tiers
third party insurance / Collision Damage Waiver (CDW)

assurance tous risques
comprehensive insurance / Full Collision Waiver (FCW)

assurance contre le vol
insurance against theft

assurance voyage
travel insurance
Going skiing abroad? Buy travel insurance online.

s'assurer (contre) / souscrire une assurance / prendre une assurance (contre)
to insure oneself (against) / to take out an insurance (against)
You must think about insuring yourself against unexpected medical expenses or loss of baggage while abroad.
We strongly advise that you take out adequate insurance before you leave to cover you for any health and medical issues, and also for theft or damage to your belongings.

assuré (n)
insured person / policy holder

assuré
insured
Your personal belongings are insured while travelling to and from your destination country when they are damaged or lost solely due to theft, robbery, assault, traffic accident or transportation company mishandling.

être bien assuré
to be properly insured

We strongly recommend that you and your party be properly insured as soon as you book your holiday.

assureur
insurer / insurance broker
Insurers are preparing for yet more claims to cover flooding, damage and repair work.

compagnie d'assurance
insurance company

conflit
dispute
Disputes relating to travel insurance claims are on the rise.

contrat
contract / agreement
A contract shall come into existence if and when we accept the booking in writing.

contrat d'assurance
insurance contract / insurance policy
Can an insurance contract be tailor-made to our needs or are they standard in form?

contrat de location
rental agreement
The rental agreement is the contract between the car hire company and the renter.
It requires the renter's signature and lists total charges and conditions of rental.
Check your rental agreement before signing!

convenu
agreed / stipulated
comme convenu
as agreed

couverture
coverage / cover
couverture d'assurance
insurance coverage / insurance cover / cover
Travellers should purchase appropriate insurance coverage against unsafe conditions, health hazards, political instability…

couverture médicale
medical cover

plafond de la couverture
limit of cover / limit of coverage

portée de la couverture
extent of cover / extent of coverage

étendre la couverture
to extend cover / to extend coverage

couvrir
to cover
No travel insurance policy will cover you for everything that might happen on your holiday. A policy will usually cover events such as personal injury and loss or theft of your possessions, as well as costs that you incur if your travel plans are disrupted.

couvrir les frais / les dépenses
to cover costs / to cover expenses
Your expenses will be entirely covered.

défalquer / déduire
to deduct
You have to deduct the deposit.

dégâts
damage
They were liable for the damage done.

dégâts des eaux
water damage
Is water damage covered by my policy?

dégâts matériels
property damage / damage to property / material damage

dommages corporels
physical injury / damages to persons

dommages et intérêts
damages
Passengers are seeking damages from airlines after suffering deep vein thrombosis (DVT).

durée
duration
A travel insurance policy should cover you for the entire duration of your trip.

engager une procédure judiciaire
to take legal action / to launch legal action
Passengers who missed their flights because of long airport queues are taking legal action after the airline made them forfeit their tickets.

exclure
to exclude
What does my insurance policy cover and exclude?

exclusion
exclusion
Carefully check all the exclusions before you decide on a travel insurance policy.

facultatif
optional

grève
strike
A crippling national transportation strike.
Workers have begun a strike that has severely disrupted the country's transport system.

se mettre en grève
to go on strike
Several hundred baggage handlers, cargo staff and other workers went on strike in support of the employees who were sacked by the catering firm.

imprévu
unexpected

les imprévus
unexpected events
The insurance policy generally covers such unexpected events as medical expenses, emergency evacuation, accidental death insurance, trip interruption...

faire face aux imprévus
to face unexpected events

inclure
to include
Our insurance includes on-piste snowboarding and skiing, off piste skiing and snowboarding provided it is not done in restricted or unsafe areas.

indemniser
to compensate

indemnisation
compensation
You are entitled to compensation.
Compensation will not be paid in case of the insured's death, if the cause of death was an illness.

demande d'indemnisation
claim / compensation claim

faire une demande d'indemnisation / réclamer des indemnités
to submit a claim for / to make a claim for / to claim / to file for compensation
to claim damages

indemnité en cas de décès
death compensation
In case of accidental death of the insured, a death compensation will be paid to the legal heirs.

intégralement
in full / fully
The sum will be repaid in full.

intégralité de la somme
full balance / whole sum / whole amount
If cancellation is not notified within 8 weeks of the holiday commencement date, you will be liable to pay the full balance.
The whole sum will have to be paid when you sign the contract.

irrecevable
invalid
I'm afraid your claim is invalid.

justificatif de paiement
receipt

manuscrit (adj)
hand-written

objets de valeur
valuable items / valuables
Avoid leaving valuables in your room.
Your valuable items such as cameras, sound equipment or mobiles may be stolen if left "unattended" in a hire car.

obligatoire
compulsory / mandatory / obligatory

se plaindre (de)
to complain (about)
The guest complained about the noise.
Airline passengers typically complain about flight delays and mishandled baggage.

plainte
complaint
The Department Of Transportation's detailed breakdown of complaint categories per airline provides an effective guide to carriers that excel and falter in various aspects of customer service.

porter plainte (contre qqn)
to lodge a complaint / to file a complaint / to file a claim (against so / for sthg)
Not all travellers are aware of how to file a complaint.
In filing a claim for property loss or damage, you must also provide a detailed description of the property along with its date of purchase and value. Bills, invoices or other proof of value are required.

police d'assurance
insurance policy / policy

All travel insurance policies have specific exclusions.
Our insurance policies can be bought online.
Our policies cover a wide range holidays from simply relaxing on the beach in Spain to bungee jumping in New Zealand.

rapatriement
repatriation

Travellers going to destinations with political instability may want to check out special travel insurance policies that provide security services and repatriation for U.S. citizens in case of war or civil disturbances.
In case of accidental death, the repatriation of remains to the place of burial in the home country will be covered.

rapatriement sanitaire
repatriation on medical grounds / medical evacuation

Travellers should take out an insurance that covers repatriation on medical grounds.
Accidents do happen and medical evacuations can be very expensive.

rapatrier
to repatriate

A traveller without an up-to-date, correctly stamped vaccination certificate may be detained in isolation at the port of arrival or repatriated.

risques
risks / hazards

évaluation des risques
risk assessment

A travel risk assessment should consider what is the preferable means of transport in view of the potential weather conditions, medical condition of the travellers, etc.

secourir
to rescue

Dozens of people had to be rescued from the site at the height of the storm yesterday.
Firefighters used hydraulic cutting gear, airbags and thermal imaging cameras to help rescue seven people.

signaler la perte de / signaler le vol de
to report the loss of / to report the theft of
I want to report the loss of my credit card.
In case of a robbery, you must report the loss to the police, transportation company, hotel, etc.,

and provide a copy of this report to Claims Departement along with your request for reimbursement.

sinistre (n)
accident / loss / damage

urgence
emergency

In an emergency that requires ambulance, police or fire services dial 999 from any telephone.

en cas d'urgence…
In the event of an emergency…
Should you encounter an emergency dial 999.

—— 2 ——
ARGENT / CHANGE / MOYENS DE PAIEMENT
Money / Foreign Exchange / Means of payment

achat
buy / purchase
Visitors can claim a refund on VAT for purchases they take home with them.

acheter
to buy / to purchase
Think twice before you buy souvenirs!
The government is warning tourists travelling abroad not to purchase souvenirs made from endangered species.

affaire
bargain
People shop for bargains abroad.
Shoppers are hunting for bargains.

une bonne affaire
a real bargain

agence bancaire
bank branch / branch
Is there a bank branch nearby?

argent liquide
cash
Carrying large amounts of cash around is insecure.

billet de banque
banknote / note / bill (US)
In the Eurozone, banknotes are printed in denominations of 5, 10, 20, 50, 100, 200 and 500 euros. The introduction of euro bills and coins has made trips in the Eurozone more convenient.

faux billets
forged notes / fake notes
Several shops have been offered forged € 20 notes to pay for small items.

bon marché
cheap / inexpensive

bureau de change
foreign exchange bureau / currency exchange kiosk

carte bancaire
bank card

carte de crédit
credit card
Credit cards are a convenient, secure and cost-effective means of payment when travelling.

change
foreign exchange / currency exchange
Currency exchange is available at many different sources, from airports and banks to travel agencies and street kiosks.

changer de l'argent
to exchange foreign currency
Foreign currency can easily be exchanged at banks, post offices, some hotels and currency exchange kiosks, which are found at international airports and most city centres.

chèque
cheque / check
He wrote a cheque for € 210.

chèques de voyage
traveller's cheques / traveller's checks
Traveler's checks are a safe form of currency to carry.

chéquier
cheque book

encaisser un chèque
to cash a cheque

faire un chèque / établir un chèque
to write a cheque

cher
costly / expensive / pricey

commission
commission
Currency exchange kiosks often have high commission rates.

comparer les prix
to compare prices
The euro has made it much easier for people to compare prices and use the banks that impose the lowest fees.

compte bancaire
bank account / account
What's your account number?
Mobile banking offers travellers a quicker way to check balances and transfer funds between accounts.

conversion
conversion

convertir
to convert
EU citizens are able to "think" in euro and understand values without having to convert into / from the old national currency.

convertisseur de devises
currency converter
A multilingual currency converter.

cours
rate
Rates are updated daily.

cours d'achat
buying rate

cours de vente
selling rate

découvert
overdraft
Authorized overdraft ≠ unauthorized overdraft

être à découvert
to go overdrawn / to be overdrawn / to have an overdraft / to be in the red
Most banks charge a fee if you go overdrawn. They are over € 150 overdrawn / they are overdrawn by € 150.

détenteur d'une carte bancaire / d'un compte en banque
cardholder / accountholder

devise
currency / foreign currency
Banks, exchange shops and hotels will lose some revenue earned from buying and selling foreign currency.
Visitors may bring in Thailand any amount of foreign currency for personal use, but the amount taken out should never exceed that declared upon entry.

devise faible
soft currency

devise forte
hard currency

distributeur automatique de billets / guichet automatique
Automated Teller Machine (ATM) / automatic teller / cash dispenser / cash point / cash machine
Automatic tellers permit users to complete basic transactions without requiring the assistance of bank personnel.

frais
fees
Buy UK pounds sterling traveler's checks before coming to London as fees will be incurred to exchange other currency traveler's checks.

frais de change
foreign exchange fees
Tourists can easily be hit with extortionate foreign exchange fees and transaction charges.

frais de transaction
transaction charges
The transaction charges for withdrawals of cash from ATMs and for shop purchases when abroad are changing.

faire payer (frais / commission)
to charge (fees / commission) / to levy (charges)

marchandage
haggling / bargaining

marchander
to haggle / to bargain
If you haggle you can get about 20 % off the asking price.

mode de paiement / de règlement
means of payment / means of settlement
Shopkeepers are reminded to check all methods of payments to ensure they are not a victim of fraud.

monnaie du pays
currency
The rand is South Africa's currency.

monnaie (petites pièces)
change
Can you spare change?

montant
amount
The amount of the transaction exceeded € 1,300.

faire opposition
to put a stop on / to stop (a payment, a cheque…)

payer / régler
to pay (for)
We recommend travellers use a credit card to pay for purchases.

payer en liquide
to pay in cash

payer par chèque
to pay by cheque

pièces de monnaie
coins
In the Eurozone, coins are minted in denominations of 1, 2, 5, 10, 20 and 50 cents, 1 and 2 euros.

retirer de l'argent
to withdraw money (from)
You can withdraw cash from the ATM outside the bank.

retrait d'argent
cash withdrawal
All ATMs are equipped for hassle-free withdrawals, fund tranfers as well as balance and transfer inquiries.

transférer de l'argent
to transfer money / to transfer funds
Travellers can check their account balances and transfer funds between accounts using their mobile phones.

transfert d'argent
money transfer / fund transfer

taux de change
exchange rate / rate of exchange
What is the current exchange rate?

variations du taux de change
exchange rate fluctuations

varier
to fluctuate

vol
theft
In case of passport loss or theft, report to the local police and the relevant embassy.

3

FORMALITÉS D'ENTRÉE ET DE SORTIE
Border formalities

---

accords de Schengen
Schengen agreement

ambassade
embassy
The embassy of India.

amende
fine / penalty
To pay a fine.
There are heavy penalties for smuggling.

animal domestique
pet
Dogs, cats and ferrets from certain countries are able to enter Britain via selected ports of entry under the pilot Pets Travel Scheme without quarantine – provided certain conditions are met.
Pets brought into Germany must have current vaccination certificates.

application (lois / mesures de sécurité…)
enforcement / application
The application of the "US VISIT" programme.

appliquer
to enforce / to apply
In order to maintain the security enforcement in airports, American authorities might apply further controls to the travellers.

se conformer (à)
to abide (by) / to comply (with)
Passengers must comply with airline regulations.

conformément à la réglementation en vigueur
in accordance with the present regulations / in compliance with the regulations now in force

contrebande
smuggling
Checks are carried out on travellers. If we stop you and ask you about your baggage, please co-operate as we need your help to prevent smuggling.
China's fashion-conscious urban young are developing a growing appetite for the cool white look of platinum jewelry. So it is hardly surprising that there is rampant smuggling of the precious metal that comes mostly from South Africa and Zimbabwe.

faire de la contrebande
to smuggle

passer / introduire des marchandises en fraude
to smuggle in goods
If you are caught smuggling prohibited goods into EU countries, you could face up to seven years in prison.

contrebandier
smuggler

contrefaçon
counterfeiting
We have to assess the magnitude and impact of counterfeiting.
Counterfeiting constitutes a dangerous threat for our health, safety and the economy.

marchandises contrefaites
counterfeit goods / products

contrôle sanitaire aux frontières
border health check

déclarer
to declare
From 15 June 2007, if you are travelling to or from a country outside the European Union, you will need to declare any sums of cash of 10,000 € or more to HM Revenue & Customs.

rien à déclarer
nothing to Declare
One passenger was stopped in the "Nothing to Declare" customs channel at London's Heathrow airport carrying a two-metre stuffed Nile crocodile.

marchandises à déclarer
goods to declare
If you have goods to declare, you must speak to a customs officer.

délivrer un visa / un passeport
to deliver a visa / a passport
Visas are delivered by embassies and consulates.

délit
crime
To avoid being the target of crime, do not wear conspicuous clothes or jewelry.

commettre un délit
to commit a crime

demande de visa / de passeport
visa application / passport application

faire une demande de passeport / de visa
to apply for a passport / a visa / to make an application for a passport / a visa
If you need to travel in less than two weeks you should make an urgent application for a new passport.
All visa applicants will have to submit their biometric data when they apply for a visa for the United Kingdom.

détaxe
duty free
Rising air traffic fuels duty free boom.

marchandises en détaxe
duty free goods

achats en détaxe
duty free purchases
Duty free purchases comprising alcoholic drinks, cosmetics and toiletries, tobacco, luxury items and food increased significantly last year.

ventes en détaxe
duty-free sales
Duty free sales figures reflect the increase in air traffic in the region.

douane
customs

douanier
customs officer
Customs officers are so thin on the ground that they are no discouragement to terrorists.

Customs officers occasionally carry out selective checks on travellers passing through the green channel.

droit de douane
customs duty
No additional VAT or customs duty will be payable on entry into the UK.

droit d'accise / accise
excise duty / excise tax

payer des droits de douane
to pay customs duty (on) / to pay duties (on)

passible de droits de douane
dutiable / liable to tax
Here's the list of dutiable goods and the respective duty rates imposed on the goods.

drogue
drug

empreintes digitales / relevé d'empreintes digitales
fingerprints / fingerscans
Under the US-VISIT programme, the US Customs and Border Protection Officer uses the digital fingerscanner to capture fingerscans. Since November 29, 2007, Homeland Security has replaced the two-fingerprint scanners with new ten-fingerprint scanners.

entrée
entry
Rules governing the entry of foreigners are subject to change and you should check with the relevant authorities.

entrer dans un pays
to enter a country
Some travellers may not be eligible to enter the United States visa free under the Visa Waiver Program.

faire entrer des marchandises dans un pays
to bring goods Into a country
What goods can I bring into Canada?

étranger
foreigner (n) / foreign (adj)

à l'étranger
abroad / overseas
Why not go abroad for the Easter holidays?

exemption de visa
visa waiver

programme d'exemption de visa
Visa Waiver Program (VWP)

With the introduction of visa free travel to citizens of 27 countries, it is now possible for many travellers to enter the United States without a visa under the Visa Waiver Program (WVP).

formalités d'entrée et de sortie
border formalities

South Africa, Zimbabwe, Zambia and Mozambique have signed an agreement to ease border formalities and smooth the passage of travellers through border posts.

formulaire
form

remplir un formulaire
to fill in a form / to fill out a form

You will be required to fill out form I-94W before entry to the USA under the Visa Waiver Program.

fouille
check / search

If items are damaged during the check you can claim compensation.

The nature of the search may take a number of forms, from a pocket search to a full strip or intimate body search.

fouiller
to search

Vehicles may be searched at the discretion of the customs officers.

A customs officer may ask to search you if he suspects that you are carrying any item liable to excise duty or tax which has not been paid – for example perfume, cigarettes, alcohol, in excess of the duty-free allowance.

fraude
fraud

frontière
border

They are hoping the new arrangements will improve effectiveness in crime detection and prevention on both sides of the border.

franchissement des frontières
border crossing

frontalier (adj)
border / frontier

Frontier zone.

immigration
immigration

officier de police / fonctionnaire du service de l'immigration
immigration officer

He should have reported to the immigration officer.

Immigration officers were told not to deport foreign students who overstay their visas, unless they have broken the law.

service de l'immigration
immigration authorities

interdire
to ban / to forbid / to prohibit

Some goods are banned or restricted by law.

nationalité
nationality

On arrival in the United Kingdom, you must show a valid national passport or other equivalent official document that satisfactorily establishes your identity and nationality.

papiers d'identité
ID / identity card / identity documents / travel documents

Biometric travel documents contain the holder's details on a tamper proof biometric chip.

pays d'accueil
host country

pays d'origine
home country / country of origin

You can contact your home country while abroad.

passeport
passport

The Identity and Passport Service has announced that young people aged 16 or 17 will be able to apply for a passport without parental consent.

If you are applying to replace a passport that has been lost, stolen or damaged, additional information may be required.

passeport biométrique
biometric passport

Is the biometric passport secure?

In March 2006, the UK launched one of the most important counter-fraud initiatives, the biometric passport.

passeport en cours de validité
valid passport / fully valid passport

A valid passport is essential for travel to destinations in this brochure.
Visitors entering Britain must be in possession of a valid passport.

passeport à lecture optique
Machine Readable Passport (MRP)
All Visa Waiver Program travellers will have to present a machine-readable passport (MRP) for visa-free entry into the United States.
The machine-readable passport benefits foreign visitors as much as it does homeland security.

passer la douane
to go through customs

passer la frontière
to cross the border
US-VISIT is a continuum of security measures that begins overseas and continues through arrival and departure from the United States to ensure the person crossing the border is the same person who received the visa.
They crossed the border into Argentina.

permis de conduire
driving licence

permis de conduire international
international driving licence / international driving permit
An International Driving Permit (IDP) is proof that you hold a valid driving licence in your home country at the date of issue of the IDP and should be carried with your domestic driver's licence.

piratage
piracy
Counterfeiting and piracy continues to be a growing threat in the European Union.

police de l'air et des frontières
border police / border force
The government has called for a new national border force, to stem the tide of foreign criminals entering the country.

prorogation
extension
He was refused a passport extension.
I apply for the extension of validity of my passport.

proroger (un visa / un passeport)
to extend (a visa / a passport)
In the UK, an adult passport can be extended for up to 10 years from the day it was issued.

A passport that was given as a result of a lost, stolen or mutilated passport will be extended by one year only.

quarantaine
quarantine / quarantine period
The animal has been released from quarantine.
The government raised the quarantine period from six to eight months after the case of a rabid dog in Kent.

en quarantaine
in quarantine

mettre en quarantaine
to quarantine / to place under quarantine
Passengers were moved to a hospital and placed under quarantine.

rapporter
to bring back
What does a footstool made out of an elephant's foot, a leopard skin waistcoat and a live scorpion have in common? They are all examples of some of the more bizarre souvenirs that people bring back from their holidays.
Every year, holidaymakers bring back a range of illegal articles, including coral, ivory, animal skins and turtle shell products, unaware that importing them is either illegal or requires a special permit.

récupérer la TVA
to reclaim VAT
Large amounts of VAT go unclaimed each year, mainly because tourists are not aware that they are entitled to reclaim VAT spent outside their own country.

réglementation
rules / regulations
If you are planning to travel into or out of the United Kingdom, there are rules about what goods you can bring with you without paying duty or VAT in the United Kingdom.

réglementations douanières
customs regulations
Before crossing the border, be sure you are aware of customs regulations.

remboursement
refund
To be able to claim a VAT refund you must complete a valid tax refund document obtained from the retailer.

remboursement de la TVA
refund on VAT / VAT refund

rembourser
to refund / to reimburse

renouvellement
renewal
Passport renewal / Visa renewal

renouveller un passeport / un visa
to renew a passport
Do you wish to renew your passport?

saisie
seizure / confiscation
The seizure comprised mainly of Nike and Adidas branded trainers and clothing which bore brand logos including Stone Island and Timberland.

marchandises saisies
seized goods / confiscated goods
Among the most commonly seized illegal goods were live parrots, snakes, lizzards, iguanas, live plants, elephant ivory and skin products, tortoises, coral...

saisir
to seize / to confiscate
Last year, European Union officials seized 250 million fake items at its borders.
Most of the confiscated items were souvenirs and traditional Chinese medicinal products, but there were live animals as well.

saisir des marchandises contrefaites
to seize counterfeit goods
Around £100,000 of counterfeit goods were seized at Heathrow airport.

sortie
exit / channel
Most UK ports and airports have three exits or "channels" (the red channel, the green channel and the blue channel). Use the blue channel if you are travelling from an EU country with no banned or restricted goods.

taxes d'aéroport
airport taxes / Airport Improvement Fees (AIFs)
Airport taxes are applied for both national and international departures.
Airport Improvement Fees are levied on departing passengers' tickets.
Passengers departing Vancouver International Airport are required to pay an Airport Improvement Fee (AIF).

TVA (taxe à la valeur ajoutée)
VAT (value added tax)
The Value Added Tax, or VAT, in the European Union is a general, broadly based consumption tax assessed on the value added to goods and services.

TVA à taux réduit
reduced-rate VAT

TVA taux zéro
zero rate
The UK applies zero rates for children's clothes and food.
Buying at zero rate VAT.

tolérances douanières
customs allowance

usage personnel
own use / personal use
If you come to the UK directly from another EU country you can bring as much alcohol and tobacco as you want providing if it is for your own use.

visa
visa
British passport holders do not need a visa to visit the United States on business, pleasure or in transit if they intend to stay in the United States for less than 90 days.

visa à l'arrivée
visa on arrival (VoA)

sans visa
visa free

visa touristique
tourist visa

visa de transit
visa transit card

4

SANTÉ
ET FORMALITÉS SANITAIRES
Health and health formalities

---

absorption / prise / dose
intake
Alcohol intake / medication intake / coffee intake. What's the recommended daily calcium intake?

allergie
allergie
At the first sign of allergy, the treatment must be interrupted, otherwise it might prove fatal.
Allergies to peanuts, shellfish and eggs may be fatal.

allergie aux fruits de mer
seafood allergy

risques d'allergies
allergy risks

allergique (à)
allergic (to)
Most allergic reactions to food are mild and limited to localised hives or swelling. The most serious symptoms are breathing difficulties and a drop in blood pressure.
He's allergic to seafood.

ampoules
blisters
Common causes of blisters include friction and burns.
Call your doctor if you see signs of infection around a blister.

analgésiques
painkillers
Painkillers are necessary for headaches, muscle pain, toothache and menstrual pain.

antibiotiques
antibiotics
Antibiotics fight bacterial infections, they do not fight infections caused by viruses.

anticoagulants
blood thinners

antiémétiques / antivomitifs
antiemetics / antiemetic drugs

antipyrétiques
antipyretics

avaler
to swallow
Antimalarial drugs must be taken with food and swallowed with plenty of water.
It's a hard pill to swallow!

bénin
benign
Altitude-related illness is an unpleasant but benign syndrome, consisting of headache, nausea, weakness and dizziness.

blesser (se) / se blesser au bras / à la jambe
to injure (oneself) / to injure one's arm / to injure one's leg

blessé
injured / wounded
Around 25 people have been injured after a coach crashed on the M4.

les blessés / les accidentés
the injured / the wounded
The injured were taken to the nearest hospital.

blessure
injury / wound

bouillir / faire bouillir
to boil
Boiling is the most reliable way to purify water.

eau bouillie
boiled water
In areas where chlorinated tap water is not available or where hygiene and sanitation are poor, you should remember that the only safe thing to drink would be tea and coffee prepared with boiled water, canned or bottled carbonated beverages.

brûlure
burn / skin burn
First-degree burn / second-degree burn

cachet / comprimé
tablet / pill
Water purification tablets can be purchased from pharmacies.
Tablets containing antihistamines are effective against allergies, itching, skin rashes and insect bites.

calmer / soulager
to relieve / to alleviate / to ease
It's always good to have something handy to relieve headache or diarrhoea.
To ease pain.

constipation
constipation
Constipation is one of the most common digestive complaints.
Constipation is best prevented with a high fiber diet and fluids.
Unfamiliar food and travel can cause constipation.

être constipé
to be constipated

coup de soleil
sunburn
Sunburn is prevented with a sunblock cream that has a high sun protection factor.
Sunburn and sun exposure should not be treated as insignificant.

attraper un coup de soleil
to be sunburnt

crème solaire écran total
sunblock cream

démangeaison
itch

qui gratte / qui démange
itchy
Itchy skin

éprouver des démangeaisons
to itch

déshydratation
dehydration
Common causes of dehydration include intense bouts of diarrhea, vomiting, fever or excessive sweating.
Watch for signs of dehydration!

déshydratation légère
mild dehydration
Mild dehydration can cause symptoms such as weakness, dizziness and fatigue.

déshydratation aigüe / sévère
Severe dehydration is a life-threatening medical emergency.

se déshydrater
to be dehydrated
Once you get food poisoning, there's little you can do except let it run its course. The most important thing is not to get dehydrated.

désinfectant (adj)
disinfecting / antiseptic

lingettes désinfectantes
antiseptic wipes
Take a skin-disinfecting agent with you to clean sores. Antiseptic wipes are also useful.

désinfecter
to disinfect
It is recommended to disinfect the wound prior to the application of a plaster.

diarrhée
diarrhea / diarrheoa
Acute diarrhea is an unpleasant digestive disorder.

diarrhée du voyageur
travellers' diarrhea (TD) / turista
Travellers' diarrhea is the most common illness affecting travellers. Each year between 20-40 % of international travellers develop diarrhea.

douleur
pain
Abdominal pain.
Dengue fever is an acute viral disease with intense headache, fever, joint and muscle pain, nausea and rash.

douloureux
painful

eau du robinet
tap water
Use bottled or sterilised water if you are concerned about the safety of the local tap water.

effets secondaires
side-effects
Side-effects include nausea, dizziness and anxiety.

entorse
sprain

entorse de la cheville / du genou / du poignet / du pouce
ankle sprain / knee sprain / wrist sprain / thumb sprain
sprained ankle / sprained knee / sprained wrist

se faire une entorse à la cheville / au genou / poignet / pouce
to sprain one's ankle / one's knee / one's wrist / one's thumb

épidémie
epidemic

épidémique (adj)
epidemic

flambée épidémique
disease outbreak
National health authorities are planning a response to an outbreak of wild poliovirus in Namibia, polio-free since 1996.
The cause of the disease outbreak is yet to be determined.

seuil épidémique
epidemic threshold

évitable
preventable
Acute Mountain Sickness is common but preventable if a sensible altitude gain is observed.

exposition au soleil
sun exposure
Long-term sun exposure increases the risk of skin cancer and causes aging of the skin.

fièvre
fever / temperature
Fever occurring in a traveller within three months of leaving a malaria-endemic area is a medical emergency and should be investigated urgently.

avoir de la fièvre
to have a temperature

fiévreux
feverish
He felt feverish.

fièvre aphteuse
foot-and-mouth disease

fièvre jaune
yellow fever
For yellow fever vaccine, you need to go to a World Health Organisation approved centre.

fracture
fracture
Classic signs of bone fracture may be pain, swelling and deformity.

se fracturer / se casser le poignet / le bras / la jambe
to break one's wrist / one's arm / one's leg

gonfler
to swell

gonflement
swelling

gouttes (yeux / oreilles)
drops (eye drops / ear drops)

grippe
flu / influenza

grippe aviaire
avian flu / bird flu

hypothermie
hypothermia

Four tourists have been hospitalized most of them suffering from frostbite and various stages of hypothermia.

infecté
infected
If the wound is infected, it will be red, weeping and sore.

s'infecter
to get infected

infection
infection
A viral infection.

insolation
sunstroke
Precautions should be taken against prickly heat and sunstroke.

intoxication alimentaire
food poisoning
Symptoms of food poisoning vary with the toxin ingested and may be gastrointestinal or allergic. Don't let food poisoning spoil your trip!

législation sanitaire
health legislation

maladie
disease / illness

maladies transmises par les moustiques / les rongeurs / la nourriture / l'eau
mosquito-borne diseases / rodent-borne diseases / food-borne diseases / water-borne diseases
Food and water borne diseases are frequent in Zimbabwe: watch out for amoebic dysentery, hepatitis A, and typhoid.

attraper / contracter une maladie
to catch / to contract / to get / to pick up a disease / an illness

transmettre une maladie
to pass on / to transmit / to spread a disease / an illness

malade
ill / sick

tomber malade
to be taken ill / to fall ill
Each year, international travellers fall ill with malaria while visiting countries where the disease is endemic. Some fall ill after returning home.

mal aux dents
toothache
What should I do if I have toothache when travelling abroad?

mal à la gorge
sore throat
He complained of a sore throat.

mal à la tête
headache
Taking a painkiller such as paracetamol usually works well to relieve a headache.
Visit your GP immediately if a severe headache lasts for more than 24 hours, and does not respond to any self-care treatment, or is accompanied by other symptoms such as blurred vision or vomiting.

mal au ventre
stomach ache / abdominal pain / tummy ache
The symptoms of constipation include stomach ache and cramps.
A complaint of tummy ache is often the way children express stress and worry.

mal de mer
seasickness
With symptoms such as nausea, stomach cramps and vomiting, seasickness can certainly put a damper on your cruise fun.

mal des transports
motion sickness / travel sickness
Motion sickness is a queasy, light-headed feeling that comes while travelling.
Travel sickness is caused by repetitive movements usually produced by a plane, a car or a boat.

être malade en voiture
to be carsick
Stop reading if you begin to feel carsick. Instead, face forward and focus on a fixed point.

médecin
doctor / physician

médecin généraliste
General Practitioner (GP)

médicaments
drugs / medicines / medications
Make sure you have enough of your usual medication for the whole trip.
Pack your medications in a separate pouch / bag to facilitate the inspection process.
Large amounts of drugs that are not for immediate use should be put in checked baggage.

médicaments prescrits / vendus sur ordonnance
prescription drugs / prescription medicines

être mordu / être piqué par
to be bitten
He was bitten by a poisonous spider when he was in Tasmania.

morsure / piqûre
bite
Reactions from a spider bite vary from a mild fever and rash to nausea.

morsure de serpent
snake bite
Never apply a tourniquet to a snake bite.
If you are bitten, move away from the snake to prevent additional bites.

piqûre d'insecte
insect bite

moustiquaire
mosquito net
Mosquito nets are excellent means of personal protection while sleeping. Nets can be used either with or without insecticide treatment.

nausées
nausea
Motion, smells and anxiety can all trigger nausea and vomiting during road, air and sea travel.

avoir des nausées
to feel queasy / to feel sick / to feel nauseated
Smells such as those of food or petrol and anxiety can make people feel queasy.

avoir un haut-le-cœur
to retch / to heave

ordonnance
prescription
Do I need a prescription?

délivrer une ordonnance
to write a prescription

exécuter une ordonnance
to fill a prescription

renouveller une ordonnance
to refill a prescription

paludisme
malaria

She contracted malaria while she was in Namibia.

traitement anti-paludéen
anti-malaria precautions
Anti-malaria precautions are strongly advised.
Anti-malaria precautions should be commenced prior to departure.

pandémie
pandemic
Three pandemics occurred in the previous century: "Spanish influenza" in 1918, "Asian influenza" in 1957, and "Hong Kong influenza" in 1968.
The pandemics of the previous century encircled the globe in 6 to 9 months, even when most international travel was by ship.

pansement
dressing / fabric plaster / dressing strips
Bandages and plasters are useful to have at hand in case an accident should happen.
Hands must be thouroughly washed before changing a dressing.
Plastic dressing strips for minor cuts and grazes.

pansement gastrique
antacid tablet / antacid gel / antacid suspension

pharmacie
pharmacy / drugstore / chemist's shop

plaie
wound / sore
Clean the wound properly.

pommade
ointment
He was given an ointment to be applied twice a day.

pommade antalgique / antibiotique / ophtalmique
analgesic ointment / antibiotic ointment / eye ointment

prescrire
to prescribe
The doctor prescribed generic drugs.

préservatif
condom
Condoms are still the best way of not getting a sexually-transmitted disease such as Aids.

prévention
prevention

mesure préventive
preventive measure / preventative measure

se protéger (de)
to protect oneself (against)

protections périodiques / serviettes hygiéniques / tampons
period protection pads / sanitary protection pads / pads / tampons

rage
rabies
In an area endemic for rabies, all unprovoked bites should be considered as a possible exposure.

répulsif anti-insectes
insect repellent
Insect repellents are applied to exposed skin or / and to clothing.
Insect repellents should be applied to provide protection at times when insects are biting.

saignement
bleeding
Anyone returning from travel to a dengue-infected area with bleeding signs should seek medical assistance.

saigner
to bleed

sedatif (n)
sedative
To take sedatives to aid sleep.
An investigation into a fatal crash at Birmingham airport found a common sedative in the blood of two US cockpit crew.

Sida
Aids

somnifères
sleeping tablets / sleeping pills
Sleeping pills will help you relax.
Sleeping tablets are prescribed to get over a bad spell of insomnia.

symptômes
symptoms
Symptoms of travel sickness include nausea and vomiting, cold sweats, excessive saliva production, yawning…
Symptoms will resolve quickly if appropriate action is taken.

thermomètre
thermometer
A small digital thermometer is handy when travelling. It will prove useful if you suspect a high temperature.

traitement
treatment
Travellers experiencing a fever after entering an area of malaria risk should consult a physician to obtain diagnosis and treatment.

traitement préventif / traitement prophylactique
preventative treatment / prophylactic treatment
You should take prophylactic treatment for teanus and malaria.

transfuser
to transfuse

transfusion sanguine
blood transfusion
For travellers, transfusion should be required only in rare and unexpected situations of massive hemorrhage.

transpirer / suer
to sweat

sueurs froides
cold sweat

sueurs nocturnes
nocturnal sweating / night sweats

trousse de secours / trousse de premiers soins
first-aid box / first-aid kit
What should a first-aid box contain?
A first-aid kit should contain emergency supplies and medication for unexpected minor illnesses or accidents.

urgence
emergency
High Altitude Cerebral Edema (HACE) is an emergency.
If signs of High altitude Cerebral Edema appear, emergency treatment is immediately required.

vaccin
vaccine
There's no effective vaccine against Dengue fever.
Supplies of vaccines and antiviral drugs – the two most important medical interventions for reducing illness and deaths during a pandemic – will be inadequate in all countries at the start of a pandemic.

vaccination
vaccination / immunisation
Immunisations must be planned ahead – allow 6 to 8 weeks before departure. Some immunisations require more than one dose.
A yellow fever vaccination certificate becomes valid 10 days after the immunisation has been given.

vaccination contre la rage / l'hépatite
rabies vaccination / hepatitis vaccination / immunisation against rabies / against hepatitis
Immunisation against hepatitis is effective 2 weeks after the one dose course.
Some countries ask for a certificate confirming vaccination against meningococcal infection.

être vacciné (contre)
to be immunized / to be vaccinated (against)
Travellers who have never been immunized against rabies and receive a suspect bite, should be vaccinated within 24-48 hours.

obligatoire / exigée
compulsory / obligatory / required / requested

conseillée / recommendée
advised / recommended

se faire vacciner contre
to get vaccinated against
You'd better get vaccinated against cholera, yellow fever and other tropical diseases if you intend to go to Africa.

carnet de vaccinations
vaccination notebook / international vaccination card
For mandatory vaccinations, you will need to get an international vaccination card signed and stamped.

certificat de vaccination
vaccination certificate
A yellow fever certificate is required if arriving from an infected area.
Yellow fever is the only infection for which the World Health Organisation supplies an international vaccination certificate.

être à jour de ses vaccins
to be up to date with shots
Irrespective of where you're travelling, children need to be up to date with their routine shots: diphtheria, whooping cough, tetanus, polio...

vertiges
dizziness
Call the doctor if dizziness comes suddenly, especially if accompanied by nausea or vomiting.

avoir des vertiges
to feel dizzy

vomissements
vomiting / throwing up / emesis
Many illnesses can cause stomach pain, nausea and vomiting.

vomir
to be sick / to vomit / to throw up
She was violently sick last night.

INDUSTRIE TOURISTIQUE
The tourism industry

accompagnateur
courier / tour escort / tour leader
Couriers are employed by coach companies or tour operators to supervise and shepherd groups of tourists participating in tours.

affluence (touristique)
influx
The influx of tourists has dropped lately.

agence de voyages
travel agency
A license is required to set up a travel agency.

agence de voyages sur internet / agence de voyages en ligne
online travel agency
Online travel agencies are rising rapidly.

agent de voyages
travel agent
Travel agents earn their revenue in the form of commission on sales.

agent de comptoir
counter clerk

allotement, contingent de places, chambres
allotment
Allotments allow immediate confirmation of bookings as a pre-negotiated number of seats / rooms are permanently held for sale.

allouer
to allocate
The client is allocated a booking reference number.

aménagements touristiques
tourist amenities
However attractive a destination, its potential for tourism will be limited unless the basic tourist amenities are provided.

attirant
alluring / attractive

attirer
to attract / to lure
The 2012 Olympic games and Paralympic games will boost the economy and attract tourists to London.

atttraits touristiques / attractions touristiques
tourist attractions
We must distinguish between natural attractions (beaches, mountains…) and man-made or purpose-built attractions (theme parks, historical buildings…).

autorisation / permis
licence / license (US)
A license is requested to set up business.

autotour
independent travel

auxiliaire (service) (adj.)
ancillary
Ancillary tourism services.

bénéfice
profit

réaliser des bénéfices
to make a profit / to turn a profit

marge bénéficiaire
profit margin
Because profit margins on long-haul travel are higher, tour operators and travel agencies have happily encouraged the long-haul trend.

besoin
need

répondre aux besoins
to meet the needs
The Managing Director spoke about the airline's efforts to meet the needs of business and pleasure travellers.

billeterie
ticketing

billet
ticket
These tickets are neither transferable nor refundable.

émettre un billet
to issue a ticket

bouder (une destination)
to shun (a country, a destination)
Countries like Cyprus and Greece were shunned by tourists during the Gulf War.

brochure
brochure / leaflet
Brochure descriptions are based on the information obtained during visits made by our staff.
A leaflet with prices and detailed itinerary is available upon request.

chèques voyage
holiday vouchers / travel vouchers

chiffre d'affaires
turnover
The annual turnover in sales of souvenirs tops £5 m.
Last summer's turnover exceeded $3 million.

cible
target
Target audience / target market.

circuit de distribution
chain of distribution
The term "chain of distribution" is used to describe the methods by which a product or service is distributed from its manufacturing source to its eventual consumers.

commission
commission (uncount / count)
Each booking made through the travel agent brings a commission.
You will get commission on top of your salary.
Travel agents work on a commission basis.

faire payer une commission
to charge a commission

payer une commission
to pay a commission

comptabilité
accountancy / bookkeeping

erreur de comptabilité
bookkeeping error

The mistake was due to a bookkeeping error. Please adjust your invoice accordingly.

système de comptabilité
accounting system
Uncertainty remains over the impact of EMU on tourism. Companies face the cost of adapting accounting systems and the loss of foreign exchange commissions.

service comptable
accounts department
Please contact our accounts department for any further information you may require.

concurrence
competition

concurrence acharnée
cut-throat competition

concurrence loyale / déloyale
fair / unfair competition

concurrent
competitor / rival
They temporarily slashed prices to fend off competitors.

être en concurrence
to compete (with)
The new regulations might enable American airlines to compete with European airlines.

conseil
advice (uncount)

conseiller / donner des conseils
to advise (so to do sthg) / to give advice
Travel agents advise prospective clients on resorts and facilities.

consommation
consumption

consommateur
consumer
Tours operators are selling dreams and their brochures must allow consumers to fantasise about their holiday, but it is also vitally important that consumers are not misled.

société de consommation
consumer society

contrat
contract

une rupture de contrat
a breach of contract
It qualifies as a breach of contract.

créer / générer / produire (emplois, revenus…)
to create / to generate (employment, income…)
Income is generated from interest, rent and profits on tourism businesses.
As well as income, tourism creates employment.

crise
crisis / slump
The continent suffered its worst tourist slump in 1991.

critères / normes / exigences
standards / requirements

satisfaire aux critères
to meet requirements / standards
Local beaches do not meet European standards of cleanliness.

croissance
growth
Tourism is a key point of growth in the economy.

croître (augmenter) (de)
to grow (by) / to increase (by) / to rise (by)
Jobs in tourism will grow by 20% in the future.

dégrader
to damage / to spoil
The environment has been irretrievably damaged.

demande
demand
Hoteliers find it hard to cope with tourist demand at peak season.

la loi de l'offre et de la demande
the law of supply and demand

dépasser / excéder
to exceed / to top
Boosted by a series of world-class sporting, cultural and historical events, the tourist industry – Europe's biggest employer – is expecting the number of visitors to equal or exceed numbers in 2010.

dépenses
expenditure / spending
Visa International commissioned a research on holiday travel expenditure in Europe last year. The report revealed that Germany had the largest holiday bill.

dépliant
folder

Could you include folders about itineraries and prices?

destination
destination

destination familiale
family-friendly destination
The USA is the family-friendliest of all destinations.

destination touristique
holiday destination / tourist destination
Its spectacular coastlines and unspoilt countryside make the West Country one of Britain's most popular holiday destinations.

détaillé / complet
comprehensive
You can get a comprehensive list of tour operators offering fully inclusive angling holiday arrangements by contacting the Tourist Board.

diminuer
to decline / to decrease / to diminish
Air fares to the USA have decreased by 20%.

diminuer (petit à petit)
to taper off
Tourism in the Alps usually tapers off after the Easter holidays and ski resorts are quiet again.

documentaire (de voyage)
travelogue

documentation touristique
travel data / travel literature
Would you have special literature about adventure travel?

économie (d'une région, d'un pays…)
economy
Portugal's economy is still largely based on tourism.
Tourism accounts for 12 % of Spain's GDP and supports over 2 million jobs.

économique
economic
Economic crisis / economic issues / economic policy…

économies
savings
In May huge savings on flights to European destinations!

économiser
to save
Tour operators are trying to save money by buying in bulk.

économique
economical (= cheap)
VFR (Visiting Friends and Relatives) remains an economical way to spend vacations.

vacances économiques
budget holidays

échelonner (paiements, vacances…)
to stagger (payment, holidays…)
The summer holidays are staggered in order to keep businesses running.

> **échelonnement / étalement**
> staggering

> **vacances échelonnées**
> staggered holidays

élastique (adj.) (demande, offre, prix)
elastic (ant.: inelastic)
Holiday travel is highly price elastic: lower prices will encourage an increase in the number of holidaymakers; business travel, however, is relatively price inelastic.

> **élasticité de la demande par rapport au prix**
> price elasticity of demand

> **élasticité du marché**
> market resilience

enjeu
stake
The stakes of this advertising campaign are pretty high.

> **être en jeu**
> to be at stake
> *Coastal development is at stake!*

étude de faisabilité
feasability study

étude de marché
market research

exercice (comptabilité)
financial year

excursionniste
day tripper / excursionist

facturation
invoicing

facture
bill / invoice
Your invoice will be sent within a week.
Please forward your invoice to the above address for payment.
Please send the invoice in duplicate.

> **dès paiement de votre facture**
> on payment of your invoice / in settlement of your invoice

> **règlement d'une facture**
> payment / settlement

> **régler une facture**
> to settle a bill / to pay a bill

> **vérifier une facture**
> to check an invoice
> *On checking the invoice, we noticed that you have omitted to deduct the discount of 10%.*

> **facturer**
> to invoive / to bill
> *Will your clients want to be billed in euros?*

familiariser
to acquaint (with)
Seminars are organized to acquaint travel agents with new programmes and selling techniques.

financer
to finance / to fund
The new convention centre is being funded both by Local Authorities and private industry.

> **financement**
> financing / funding

florissant
booming / flourishing / thriving
Tourism in Ireland is booming / The Irish tourist industry is thriving.

flux (touristique)
flow
The flow of American visitors has increased steadily.

formation
training

> **stage de formation (en agence)**
> in-training programme
> *Most travel agencies offer in-training programmes.*

fréquentation (touristique)
tourist attendance
As prosperity has put exotic travel destinations within the reach of many Europeans, ski resorts have suffered declines in attendance.

gamme / éventail
array (of) / range (of)
This resort offers a wide range of activities to suit all tastes.

bas de gamme
down-market / downscale

haut de gamme
up-market / upscale
The European tourist industry is advised to move upmarket and offer high quality services.

industrie
industry (uncount)
Tourism is now a major industry which accounts for over 5% of the world trade.

industrie de l'hotellerie
hotel industry

industrie touristique
tourist industry / travel industry / tourism industry
From airphones on planes to Internet access in hotels, the information age is revolutionizing the travel industry.

intermédiaire (n)
middleman

par l'intermédiaire de
through
It's best to book through a travel agent.

investissement
investment
There has been massive foreign investment in the tourist industry.

investir
to invest
The Turkish government has invested $220 million to build a new chain of sewage-treatment plants.

investisseur
investor
Investors are supporting the development project of the site.

jumelage (ville)
town twinning

A fantastic boom has been given to international tourism by the town twinning movement.

lancer un nouveau produit
to launch a new product
Underpricing a holiday is probably a good means to launch it.

frais de lancement
set-up costs

loisirs
leisure (uncount)
Leisure is an area of free choice and discretionary spending strongly influenced by national differences in climate, geography, culture and heritage.

société de loisirs
leisure society

équipements de sports et de loisirs
recreational facilities

main-d'œuvre
labour force / workforce

à fort coefficient de main-d'œuvre
labour-intensive
A labour-intensive industry.
The tourist industry is labour-intensive. This is a common feature of service industries.

marché
market
In the U.K., golf equipment is the largest sports equipment market with annual turnover of £175 million.
It is essential to define the market you're aiming at for each product.

marché des voyages
travel market

marché des voyages vendus en ligne
online travel market
The Centre for Regional Tourism and Research has found that in 2007, European online travel sales increased by 24 % to £37.2 billion, accounting for 19.4 % of the market. Last year the online travel was worth £29.9 billion.

exploiter un marché
to tap a market

part de marché
market share
This tour operator commands a 30% share of the market for inclusive holidays.

pénétrer un marché
to break into a market

A foreign company would find it hard to break into the U.K. market, since most of its big travel companies combine tour operator and travel agency functions.

segment de marché
market segment

Inland cruising is particularly popular among the older segments of the market.

mercatique
marketing

agence de commercialisation
marketing board / marketing bureau

To produce a coordinated strategy for the promotion of tourism, several cities have opted for the formation of a marketing board made up of representatives from both the public and the private sectors.

stratégie de marketing
marketing strategy

Their marketing strategy development was very efficient.

métiers du tourisme
careers in tourism / jobs in tourism

niveau de vie
standard of living

The standard of living is usually held to be determined by the quantities of goods and services (including leisure) consumed.

objectif (n)
aim / goal / objective

Our objective is to provide a very upmarket, quality airline which offers unique and distinctive service.

option
option

prendre une option
to make a provisional reservation / to take out an option

ordinateur
computer

Availability is checked on the computer.

entrer des données dans l'ordinateur
to key data into the computer

Organisation Mondiale du Tourisme (OMT)
World Tourism Organisation (UNWTO)

The World Tourism Organization, a specialized agency of the United Nations, is the leading international organization in the field of tourism.

parc à thème
theme park

Theme parks such as Eurodisney or Thorpe Park provide scope for a full day's entertainment.

planification touristique
tourist planning

politique touristique
tourist policy

For the most part, tourist policy is defined and implemented through national tourist boards.

définir une politique
to define a policy / to lay down a policy

mettre en œuvre une politique
to apply a policy / to implement a policy / to carry out a policy

pouvoir d'achat
purchasing power / buying power / spending capacity (US)

prestataire de service
service provider / service supplier

prestation
service

Tourism demand is met by the concentrated effort of a wide range of tourist services.

offrir des prestations
to provide services

Tourism is not a single industry but rather a group of related entreprises that provide services to the travelling public.

prêt (n) (somme prêtée)
loan

The International Development Association (IDA) offers interest-free or low-rate loans.

solliciter un prêt
to apply for a loan

accorder un prêt
to grant a loan

Governments aid the private sector by granting loans at preferential rates of interest for development schemes which are in keeping with government policy.

prévoir
to forecast / to foresee / to predict
Footwear specialists have detected the early signs of a boom in recreational walking, and foresee an increasing demand for walking and hiking shoes.

prix / tarifs
fares / prices / rates
Fares are heavily discounted.

prix attrayants
compelling prices

prix réduits
cut rates / discount fares / reduced prices / slashed prices

rapport qualité-prix
value for money
This tour will give you unrivalled value for money.

casser les prix
to slash prices / to undercut prices

guerre des prix
price war
The price war among budget airlines was stepped up with the launch of Buzz which flies from Stansted to major European cities.

produit
product
New products such as artificial ski slopes and indoor tropical swimming paradises have become increasingly popular.

produit intérieur brut (PIB)
gross domestic product (GDP)
The Maldivian economy is based on tourism and fishing. Tourism brings in about $450 million a year. Tourism and related services contributed 28% of GDP in 2007.

produit national brut (PNB)
gross national product (GNP)

professionnel (adj.)
professional
Since tourism is one of the world's largest industry, the role of the travel agent has become more and more professional.

professions et catégories socio-professionnelles (PCS)
socio economic classification (NS-SEC)
Since 2001 the National Statistics Socio-economic Classification (NS-SEC) has been used for all official statistics and surveys. It has replaced Social Class based on Occupation (SC, formerly Registrar General's Social Class) and Socio-economic Groups (SEG).

profiter (de) / exploiter
to capitalize (on) / to cash in (on)
Tour operators did their best to capitalize on new tourist trends.

promouvoir
to foster / to promote
The Tourist Boards' main objective is to foster tourism within a country.
The European Commission has earmarked €50,000 to promote Europe as a tourist destination.

promotion touristique
tourist promotion

promotionnel / publicitaire
promotional
The promotional efforts of both government and private sector have greatly helped to attract more tourists.
Our promotional budget has increased by 10%.

tarif promotionnel
incentive fare

publicité (gén.)
advertising
The functional responsibilities of a national tourist board include advertising, sales promotion and public relations activities directed at home and overseas markets.

publicité (une)
ad / advert / advertisement
Here's an eye-catching advertisement to promote holidays in France.

campagne publicitaire / campagne publicitaire intensive
advertising campaign / advertising blitz

faire de la publicité
to advertise
Governments should advertise less popular attractions and regions while promoting the off-season.

recettes
receipts
Receipts from tourism grew by some 37% last year.
America still dominates in term of tourist receipts.

recherche
research (uncount)

faire de la recherche
to do research
Tourist Boards do research in order to get in-depth knowledge of holiday tastes.

relié (à)
connected (with) / linked (to, with)
Most agencies are linked to terminals which provide information on departures, seat availability from the computers of major airlines.

rembourser
to refund
Lost tickets are neither refunded nor replaced.

remboursement
refund
There are limited refunds on cancellation on most economy tickets.

non remboursable
non-refundable (ant.: refundable)

rentable
profitable
According to a survey, French hotels were the most profitable in Europe before tax.

rentabililté
profitability
Hotels in Austria, probably reflecting their proximity to eastern Europe, experienced a significant increase in profitability-per-room.

seuil de rentabilité
break-even point
They failed to reach the break-even point.

rentrer dans ses frais
to break even
Hoteliers broke even despite the perceptible drop in the influx of tourists.

représenter
to account (for)
Cyprus was badly hit by the Gulf Crisis as tourism accounts for 22% of its Gross Domestic Product.

répondre aux exigences
to meet demands
Tour operators always do their utmost to meet customers' demands.

réputation
reputation
Our reputation is based on providing quality holiday and good service.

réservation
booking / reservation
Sophisticated reservation systems involve the use of computers.

réservation sur internet / réservation en ligne
online booking, online reservation / internet booking, internet reservation
Internet bookings account for fewer than 5% of total hotel reservations but are expected to grow rapidly.
Online booking is attractive to the hotel industry because it has the potential to reduce distribution costs dramatically.

centrale de réservation
reservation centre

service de réservation
booking service / reservation service
The UK tourist offices provide a booking service called "Book A Bed Ahead" (BABA) for hotels and farmhouse accommodation through their Tourist Information Centres.

système de réservation électronique
computer reservation system (C.R.S.)
It's a computer system that allows airfares, accommodation, vehicle rentals and touring products to be booked.

réserver / effectuer une réservation en ligne
to make an online booking / to book online
Accor, Europe's largest hotelier and Granada group's Forte Hotels launched an internet joint venture enabling customers to make online bookings at their hotels.

prévoir une augmentation des réservations en ligne
to expect a growth in /of online bookings

revenu
income / revenue
Tourism is the third most important source of revenue in the Falklands, after the traditional staples, fishing and wool.

revenu disponible
disposable income
The disposable income is the total income of households less income tax and national insurance contributions.

tranche des revenus élevés
high-bracket income (ant.: low-bracket income)

répercuter (hausse, baisse)
to pass sth on (to sb)
With the end of the $ 6.8 billion duty-free market, the loss of airport revenues will be passed on to passengers.
The newfound profitability of the industry is mostly explained by the failure of airlines to pass the fuel savings on to the customers.

saison
season

haute saison / basse saison
high season, peak season / low season, off-peak season

saisonnier
seasonal
Hotels and restaurants hire a lot of seasonal workers.

segments porteurs
growth sectors

solde (comptabilité)
balance

subventions
subsidies / financial aid
Governments contribute to tourism growth through the provision of financial aid to tourism projects.

subventionner
to subsidize / to provide financial aid
Subsidized recreational travel is called social tourism.

accorder des subventions
to grant subsidies
During the Gulf War, governments granted travel companies subsidies to tide them over the bad period.

sur-mesure, à la carte
tailor-made
Tailor-made packages, tailor-made tours.

taxe
tax

T.V.A.
V.A.T. (Value Added Tax)
The V.A.T. (Tour Operators) Order 1987 came into force in 1988 and imposes taxation on profit margins for any tours between EU countries.

T.V.A. comprise
V.A.T. included / including V.A.T. / inclusive of V.A.T.

T.V.A. non comprise
V.A.T. excluded / excluding V.A.T. / exclusive of V.A.T.

tourisme
tourism / tourist trade
Tourism is an industry that is still growing significantly. It provides people with the choice of a variety of occupations that may require many different kinds of skills.

tourisme de l'espace
space tourism
The Russians broke into space tourism in 2004 when California millionaire Dennis Tito paid them 20 million dollars for a rocket ride to fame and the International Space Station.

tourisme industriel et technique
industrial tourism

tourisme de loisirs
recreational tourism (ant.: business tourism)

tourisme de masse
mass tourism
As Europe enjoys – and endures – another season of mass tourism, hospitality is fast becoming an exercise in damage control.

tourisme médical
medical tourism
Medical tourism is booming as patients look abroad for cheap, fast treatment, often combined with a holiday afterwards. Countries that actively promote medical tourism include Cuba, Costa Rica, Hungary, India, Israel, Jordan, Lithuania, Malaysia and Thailand.

tourisme de mémoire
heritage tourism

tourisme macabre / tourisme sombre
dark tourism / grief tourism / disaster tourism
Grief tourism can be defined as the act of travelling to the scene of a tragedy or disaster

(e.g. Arlington National Cemetery).
Lonely Planet defines dark tourism as "Travel to sites associated with death, disaster and depravity." Examples of dark destinations include Auschwitz-Birkenau concentration camps, South Africa's apartheid museum and Robben Island prison, Vietnam's Ho Chi Minh trail, the Tuol Sleng Killing Fields outside Phnom Penh; Rwanda's genocide memorials, Katrina tours of New Orleans and New York's Ground Zero.

tourisme social
social tourism
According to the International Bureau of Social Tourism (BITS), social tourism is "all the concepts and phenomena resulting from the participation in tourism of low-income sectors of the population, made possible through well-defined social measures".
The International Bureau of Social Tourism (BITS) has been active since 1963 as a base for the study of social tourism.

tourisme urbain
urban tourism

tourisme vert
green holidays / green vacations

touristique
tourist
Spain re-evaluated its tourist policy in the late 1980s when it became locked into price wars for lower-spending mass tourists.

touristique (péjoratif)
touristy

touriste
tourist / sightseer / visitor

faire du tourisme
to go sightseeing / to go on a sightseeing tour / to tour (a region, a country).

vacances
holidays / vacations (US)
Not all of us want to spend our holidays lying on a beach; some of us want vacations that turn our mind on, not off.

être en vacances
to be on holiday / to be on vacation (US) / to holiday / to vacation (US)
The Spanish spend more money on holidays than any other Europeans, yet they are the least adventurous, preferring to holiday at home.

vacances chez des amis / dans la famille
VFR (Visiting Friends and Relatives) / VFR travel
The VFR market is a substantial and growing one in tourism.

vacancier
holiday-maker / vacationer (US)
Mediterranean resorts now have to compete for European holiday-makers with Florida and Barbados.

vendre en ligne
to sell online

ventes de voyages en lignes
online travel sales
Online travel sales are taking off.

vivre du tourisme
to live off tourism
With 2 million people living off tourism, it is easy to understand why the government is urgently trying to head off the disaster.

voyage
journey / trip / voyage (= journey by boat only)
They went on a trip to the unspoiled islands of St. Kitts and Nevis.
There is a set of beautiful twin sisters in the Caribbean, which Christopher Colombus stumbled upon in 1493 during his voyage to the New World.

partie d'un voyage
leg of a trip
The last leg of our boat trip was fantastic.

carnet de voyage
travel documents

voyage organisé, « forfait »
I.T. (Inclusive Tour) / G.I.T. (Group Inclusive Tour) / package tour (ant.: independent tour)
A package tour is an arrangement by which transport and accommodation is purchased by the tourist at an all-inclusive price.

mini-séjour
short break
The short break market is booming!

voyager
to make a trip / to travel
They travelled round the world.

voyager à l'étranger
to travel overseas

avoir beaucoup voyagé
to be well travelled

voyageur
traveller
She's a seasoned traveller.

voyagiste
tour operator / packager

COMMUNICATION
Communication

— 1 —
CORRESPONDANCE
Writing

---

accepter (offre / emploi)
to accept / to take up

annonce
advertisement / ad
With reference to your advertisement placed in The Guardian, I would like to apply for the position of hotel manager.

candidat
applicant

candidature
application
I hope you will consider my application favourably.

poser sa candidature à un emploi
to apply for a job / for a position

commande par téléphone
telephone order

concernant
about / concerning / regarding

conclure / terminer une lettre
to close off a letter

conditions
terms
We hope you will find these terms satisfactory.

conditions de paiement
terms of payment / payment terms
Could you please let us know your terms of payment?
Could you specify your payment terms?

conditions et modalités
terms and conditions

confirmation
confirmation

confirmer
to confirm
Could you please confirm your date of arrival?

veuillez confirmer par lettre / par écrit
kindly confirm in writing / please confirm in writing

contacter
to get in touch with / to contact
Please contact us if you require further details.
I am contacting you regarding your reservation.

N'hésitez pas à nous contacter pour tout renseignement complémentaire
Should you require any further information, please do not hesitate to contact us.

courriel
e-mail
Thank you for your e-mail of February 9th.

courrier
mail

dans l'attente de votre prochain courrier
I am looking forward to hearing from you soon.

curriculum vitae / CV
curriculum vitae / résumé / data sheet
Please find enclosed my curriculum vitae.

date
date

date d'arrivée
arrival date / date of arrival

date de départ
departure date / date of departure

datée / en date du
dated

délai
deadline

dans les meilleurs délais
as soon as possible / in the nearest future

respecter un délai
to meet the deadline

demande
request

demande de documentation
request for travel literature

demande d'information
enquiries

demande de renseignements concernant une facture
invoice inquiry

sur demande
upon request

à la disposition de qqn
at someone's disposal
We are at your disposal for any further questions.

se tenir à la disposition de qqn
to remain at someone's disposal
I remain at your entire disposal.

nous nous tenons à votre entière disposition pour tout renseignement complémentaire
we remain at your entire disposal for any further information you may require

embaucher
to hire / to give someone a job

entretien
interview
I remain at your disposal for an interview at your convenience.

entretien d'embauche
job interview

entretien téléphonique
telephone conversation

excuses
apologies
We offer our sincere apologies for this most unfortunate error.
Please accept our sincere apologies for any inconvenience this may cause.

s'excuser
to apologise (for)
We apologise for the delay in replying to your e-mail.

Let me apologise for the inconvenience you experienced last weekend.

fax
fax
Thank you for your fax. We have noted your time of arrival.

faire le nécessaire
to make the necessary arrangements
If you let us know your requirements, we'll make the necessary arrangements.

faire savoir à qqn
to let someone know
Will you let us know at your earliest convenience whether these terms are acceptable?

veuillez nous faire savoir dès que possible si ces conditions vous conviennent
Will you let us know at your earliest convenience whether these terms are acceptable?
Would you be so kind as to let us know if these terms are acceptable?

formulaire
form

remplir un formulaire
to fill in a form / to fill out a form
The application form for the training course must be filled in online.

formules d'introduction
opening salutations / openings
The standard opening for formal correspondence is Dear.

Cher Monsieur / Chère Madame
Dear Sir / Dear Madam

Cher Monsieur X / Chère Madame X
Dear Mr X / Dear Mrs X

Messieurs
Dear Sirs (GB) / Dear Gentlemen (US)

formules de politesse
closing salutations / closures

cordialement
kind regards

bien cordialement
kindest regards / best wishes

veuillez agréer l'expression de mes salutations distinguées / je vous prie de croire en l'expression de mes sincères salutations
yours faithfully / yours truly / yours sincerely

joindre
to enclose / to attach
I have attached my résumé and look forward to hearing from you at your earliest convenience.

ci-joint
enclosed / attached
Please find enclosed the quotation that you requested.

veuillez trouver ci-joint...
please find enclosed... (letter) / please find attached... (e-mail)
Please find enclosed the travel literature presently available.

fichier joint
attachement

pièce jointe
enclosure

lettre
letter

lettre de candidature
job application letter

lettre d'excuse
apology letter

lettre de motivation
cover letter / covering letter

lettre de réclamation
complaint letter

lettre de recouvrement
collection letter

lettre de relance
follow-up letter

lettre de remerciements
thank you letter / letter of thanks

letter type
model letter

malentendu
misunderstanding

afin d'éviter tout malentendu
in order to prevent any misunderstanding

modalités
arrangements
We hope that these arrangements will be suitable and we look forward to hearing from you.

noter
to note

veuillez noter que
please note that

objet (de la lettre / du courriel)
subject / purpose (of the letter / of the e-mail)

se permettre de
to take the liberty of
We are taking the liberty of enclosing our current price-list.

présentation de la lettre
letter layout
Adopt a letter layout that is clear and consistent.

recevoir (lettre / courriel / fax)
to receive
I sent the tickets to you this morning by overnight mail. You should receive them no later than tomorrow.

accuser réception de
to acknowledge receipt of
I am pleased to acknowledge receipt of your letter.

j'accuse réception de votre courrier du 21 septembre
I acknowledge receipt of your letter dated September 21st.

réclamation
complaint
We have received quite a few complaints from our customers.

recommander
to recommend
I can recommend Ms X without any reservations.

reconnaissant
grateful
I would be grateful if you could return my deposit.

rédiger une lettre
to write a letter

refuser (offre / emploi)
to refuse / to turn down

regret
regret

j'ai le regret de vous informer que
I regret to inform you that / I am sorry to inform you that
We regret to inform you that we will be forced to cancel your reservation if we do not receive payment within three days.

répondre
to answer / to reply

réponse
answer / reply

dans l'attente d'une réponse / de vous lire
looking forward to hearing from you

une réponse rapide nous obligerait
an early reply would be appreciated

sauf réponse de votre part
unless we hear from you to the contrary

signature
signature

signer
to sign
Please sign below.

stage
training course / training session
Full attendance at the training session is compulsory.

faire un stage
to go on a training course / to attend a training session

suite à...
following... / further to... / with reference to...
With reference to your e-mail...
Further to our telephone conversation...

suite à votre lettre du...
following your letter of... / further to your letter of...

sous huitaine
within a week

sous pli séparé
under separate cover

2
TÉLÉPHONE
Telephone

---

abonné
telephone subscriber
A telephone subscriber in the UK can choose not to receive direct marketing phone calls. Companies who do not respect the subscriber's choice can be fined.

agenda
diary
Let me have a look at Mr Field's diary.

annuaire
phone directory / phone book

pages jaunes
yellow pages

ne pas être dans l'annuaire
to be ex-directory / to be unlisted
With almost half of them choosing to be ex-directory, it seems that Britons just don't want to be called at home.

appel téléphonique
phone call

appel international
overseas call / international call

appel en PCV
reverse charge call / collect call

clavier téléphonique
telephone keypad

codes et indicatifs téléphoniques
country codes / area codes / city codes
Country codes must be dialled to reach a telephone number in another country.

composer un numéro de téléphone
to dial a phone number
In case of emergency, dial 999.
To call from the USA to the UK you have to dial 01+44+ local number.
Sorry, I think I have dialled the wrong number.

conversation téléphonique
telephone conversation
To start a telephone conversation.

être coupé
to be cut off / to be disconnected

épeler
to spell
Could you spell your name please?
What's the name again, please? Would you spell it?

indisponible
unavailable
I am afraid Mr Mortimer is unavailable at the moment.

joindre qqn / contacter qqn
to reach someone / to get through to someone / to get in touch with
I have been trying to get through to the hotel manager all morning.
You can reach me at 06 07 08 09 10.
Couldn't I get through to him by calling another number?
Please contact me at your earliest convenience.

être en ligne
to be on another call / to be on another line
I am sorry but Mr Nutt is on another call. Can I take your name and phone number?

message
message
Can I take a message?
I received your message yesterday concerning an interview time.

laisser un message
to leave a message
If you'd like to leave a message, please do so after the beep. We'll get back to you as soon as possible.
Please telephone ahead to confirm date availabilities. If there is no answer please leave a message.

prendre un message
to take a message

transmettre un message
to pass on a message
I'll pass your message on. Thank you for calling.

messagerie vocale
voice mail

numéro de téléphone
phone number
What's your phone number?
I am afraid you have got the wrong number!

numéro vert
toll-free number / freephone number

vous êtes bien au (+ numéro tel)
you have reached (+ phone number)

quel numéro demandez-vous ?
what's the number you are calling?

objet de l'appel
reason for the call

occupé (ligne)
engaged / busy (line)
The line is engaged / the line is busy.
I have tried to get through several times but it's always engaged.

parler distinctement
to speak distinctly

parler plus fort
to speak up
I am sorry, I can't hear you very well. Could you speak up please?

passer un appel à qqn / mettre en communication / mettre en ligne
to put someone through (to)
Could you put me through to 06 34 71 74 18?
Could you put me through to the hotel manager please?

je vous le / la passe
putting you through / I put you through to him / her / I'll connect you

poste
extension

ne quittez pas !
hold the line please! / hold on! / just a moment please!

veuillez ne pas quitter
Could you hold the line please? Can you hold the line a moment?

rappeler
to call back / to return a call
Could you call back later?

récapituler
to repeat back
I repeat back: a first class seat to Cape Town, leaving Paris Charles de Gaulle on June 22^(nd) at 11p.m.

rendez-vous
appointment

annuler un rendez-vous
to cancel an appointment
I am calling to cancel the appointment made for next Saturday.

fixer une date de rendez-vous
to arrange a time for an appointment

prendre un rendez-vous
to make an appointment
I am afraid Mr Shuttleworth can't make an appointment at such short notice. Can you suggest another date and time?

reporter un rendez-vous
to postpone an appointment / to put off an appointment

renseignements téléphoniques
directory enquiries

répéter
to repeat
Could you repeat the number please?

répondre au téléphone
to answer a call

répondeur téléphonique
answering machine

SMS / texto
SMS (Short Message Service) / text message

standard
swithchboard
The swithchboard controls all the incoming calls and lines to the various departments.

standardiste
swithchboard operator

service téléphonique
telephone service
We provide a 24-hour telephone service.

téléphone
telephone / phone

téléphone portable
cellphone / mobile phone

téléphone sans fil
cordless phone

téléphone à touches
touch tone telephone

téléphoner / appeler
to phone / to call / to ring
The manager phoned while you were out.
Please call us using one of the numbers listed above.
Feel free to call our toll-free number

téléphoner en PCV
to call reverse charge / to place a collect call
To call reverse charge, simply dial 0800 followed by the numbers that spell REVERSE on the telephone keypad.
Ask the operator to place a collect call to your home number.

n'hésitez pas à nous appeler à ce numéro
feel free to call us at this number

qui est à l'appareil ?
who's calling please? / who's speaking please? / may I say who's calling? (formal)

X à l'appareil
this is X speaking / X speaking

tonalité
dial tone / dialling tone

Index français

A

abbatiale / abbaye 73
abonné 130
abordable / accessible 38
abrité 30
absorption / prise / dose 108
accepter (offre / emploi) 127
accès internet 61
accident d'avion 80
accident de voiture 94
accompagnateur 116
accorder les mets et les vins 51
accords de Schengen 104
accoster 91
accueil 23
achat 101
aérien 80
aérodrome 80
aérogare 80
aéroglisseur 91
aéroport 80
affaire 101
affaires 57
affluence (touristique) 116
affréter (un avion) 80
agence bancaire 101
agence de voyages 116
agenda 130
aigre-doux 45
air marin 30
aire de jeux pour enfants 25
aire de repos 94
aire de stationnement 94
algues 30, 38

allergie 109
allotement, contingent de places, chambres 116
allouer 116
alpinisme 7
altipiste / altiport 7
altitude 7
altitude de croisière 80
amarré 30
amarrer 91
amateur de vins 51
ambassade 104
améliorer 38
aménagement du littoral 30
aménagements pour les handicapés 25
aménagements touristiques 116
amende 94, 104
ampoules 109
amuse-gueule 45
analgésiques 109
ancre 30, 91
animal domestique 23, 104
animé 73
annonce 127
annuaire 130
annulation / annuler 25
annulation de voyage 98
annuler (une réservation, un vol) 80
anse 30
antibiotiques 109
anticoagulants 109
anticyclone 16
antiémétiques / antivomitifs 109
antipyrétiques 109

antiquités 73
appareiller (bateau) 91
appartement 27
appel téléphonique 130
appellation 51
appétissant 45
application (lois / mesures de sécurité…) 104
après-ski 7
aquarium 30
arc-en-ciel 16
archipel 30
architecture 73
argent liquide 101
arrhes 25
arrière-pays 62
art 73
artère principale 94
artisanat 62
artistique 73
ascenseur 25
ascension 7
assaisonnement 45
assistance 98
association à but non lucratif 62
association humanitaire 62
assurance 98
assurer (s') (contre) / souscrire une assurance / prendre une assurance (contre) 98
atelier 59
atmosphère 16
atoll 30
atout 73
atténuer 62
atterrir 80

E

H

habitant 76
habitudes alimentaires 41
hameau 10
harceler les animaux 67
harnais 10
hébergement 23
hébergement agréé 23
héberger 28
héliographe 18
héliport 10
hémisphère 18
heure d'été 18
heures de pointe 95
hôpital 76
horaire 84
horaires / grille horaire 89
horaires d'ouverture / heures
    d'ouverture 76
hors des sentiers battus 67
hostellerie 28
hôtel 23
hôtel de ville 76
hôtelier (adj.) 23
hôtelier (n) 23
hôtesse (de l'air) 84
hub, plate-forme de
    correspondances,
    de connexions 84
hublot 92
huile 41
humide 19
hydrothérapie 41
hygiène 67
hypothermie 111

I

identité 67
île 33
immigration 106

impact / effet 67
impasse 95
imperméable (adj) 10
imprévu 100
imprimante 61
inclure 100
indemniser 100
indicateur horaire 89
indisponible 131
industrie 120
industrie de l'hotellerie 120
industrie touristique 120
inexploré 67
infecté 111
inondation 19
inscription 60
insipide 48
insolation 111
institut de beauté 41
intégralement 100
intégrité 67
interdire 67, 84, 106
intermédiaire (n) 120
internet haut débit 25
intoxication alimentaire 111
investissement 120
inviter qqn au restaurant 48
iode 33
irrecevable 100
itinéraire 92

J

jardin 48
jardin botanique 76
jardin paysagé 76
jardin public 76
jardin tropical 76
jardins suspendus 76
jetée 33
joindre 129
joindre qqn / contacter qqn 131

jumelage (ville) 120
jumelles 10
jus de fruits 48
justificatif de paiement 100

K

kilométrage illimité 95
kinésithérapeute 41
kiosque 89
klaxonner 95

L

lac 10
lancer un nouveau produit 120
langouste 33
langue 67
langue de travail 60
large / haute mer 33
latitude 19
lèche-vitrine 76
législation sanitaire 111
légumes 48
lettre 129
lever (se) 19
liaison (aérienne) 84
liaison feroviaire 89
libérer (une chambre) 26
libre (chambre) 26
lieu 60
lieux d'intérêt touristique 76
ligne (d'horizon, des toits…) 76
ligne à grande vitesse 89
lignes de banlieue 89
lignes intérieures 84
lignes régulières 84
lignes secondaires 89
limitation de vitesse 95
limiter 67
lit à baldaquin 25
littoral 33

139

P

Index anglais

A

abate (to) / subside (to) 16

abbey / abbey church 73

abide (to) (by) / comply (to) (with) 104

aboard / on board 81

aboard / on board / shipboard 91

about / concerning / regarding 127

abseil (to) 9

accept (to) / take up (to) 127

access road 94

accident / loss / damage 101

accommodate (to) 92

accommodation / lodging (US) 23

account (to) (for) 123

accountancy / bookkeeping 117

acquaint (to) (with) 119

admission charge / entrance fee 75

advertisement / ad 127

advertising 122

advice (uncount) 117

affordable 38

after-dinner liqueur 53

after-ski / après-ski 7

ageing / aging / maturing 55

agreed / stipulated 99

Aids 113

aim / goal / objective 121

air 80

air congestion / backup (US) 83

air pass 84

air space 83

air ticket / plane ticket 81

air transport 86

aircraft (pl. aircraft) / airplane / plane 80

air-fare 86

airfield 80

air-hostess / cabin attendant (C.A.) / flight attendant 84

airline 82

airlink / link 84

airport 80

airport taxes / Airport Improvement Fees (AIFs) 108

airstrip / runway 85

air-traffic 86

air-traffic controler 86

alarm 90

algae / seaweed 38

allergie 109

allocate (to) 116

allotment 116

alluring / attractive 116

amenities 58

amount 103

anchor 30, 91

ancillary 116

answer (to) / reply (to) 130

answer a call (to) 132

answering machine 132

antibiotics 109

anticyclone 16

antiemetics / antiemetic drugs 109

antipyretics 109

antiques 73

apologies 128

appellation 51

appetizer 45

appetizing (≠ unappetizing) 45

applicant 127

application 127

appointment 132

approved accommodation 23

aquarium 30

archipelago 30

architecture 73

area / district / neighborhood (US) 78

arise (to) (wind) / lift (to) (fog) 19

arrangements 129

array (of) / range (of) 120

art 73

art gallery 75

artificial ski slopes / dry ski slopes 12

artistic 73

artistic wealth / artistic resources 73

ascent 7

ashore / on-shore 93

assessment / evaluation 66

asset / draw / drawing card 73

assistance 98

at someone's disposal 128

atmosphere 16

atoll 30

attend a conference (to) 60

attendance 60

attendee 60

audio-visual equipment (AV) 61

auditorium 59

aurora australis / southern polar lights 16

aurora borealis / northern polar lights 16

authenticity 62

Automated Teller Machine (ATM) / automatic teller / cash dispenser / cash point / cash machine 103

availability / available 26

avalanche / snowslide 7

avenue / parkway (US) 94

awaken tourists to (to) / make tourists aware of (to) / raise tourists awareness of (to) 71

awareness / consciousness 70

B

baby-sitting service 25

backcountry / hinterland 62

baggage (US) / luggage (sg. a piece of luggage) 81

baggage check-in / luggage check-in 83

baggage reclaim 85

balance 124

balneotherapy / spa therapy 38

ban (to) / forbid (to) / prohibit (to) 84, 106

ban (to) / prohibit (to) / forbid (to) 67

bank (river) / shore (lake) 13

bank account / account 102

bank branch / branch 101

bank card 102

banknote / note / bill (US) 102

bargain 101

bargaining / haggling 68

barge 93

barometer 16

barrel / cask 54

basilica 74

bath 38

bathing / sea bathing 31

bathing hut 31

baths 38

bay 30

be airlifted (to) 10

be airsick (to) 80

be bitten (to) 112

be carsick (to) 112

be cut off (to) / be disconnected (to) 131

be held (to) (at, in) / take place (to) (at, in) 76

be on another call (to) / be on another line (to) 131

beach 35

beach hut 31

beachcomb (to) 36

beauty salon / beauty parlour 41

"Bed and Breakfast" 27

bedroom / room 24

beer 51

bend / curve 97

beneficial (to) 38

benefits 39

benign 109

berth 92

beverages / drinks 45

bill / check (US) / tab (US) 45

bill / invoice 119

binding 9

binoculars 10

black box / flight recorder 81

bleeding 113

blind-alley / cul-de-sac 95

blisters 109

blood thinners 109

blow (to) 21

board (to) (a plane) / embark (to) / get on (to) (a plane) 82

board (to) (a train) / get on (to) (a train) (ant. to get off) 89

board (to) / embark (to) / go on board (to) 92

boast (to) 78

boat / ship (fem.) 91

body wrap 40

boil (to) 109

booked up / fully booked 82

booking / reservation 26, 58, 123

booking service / reservation service 123

bookstall / newsstand (US) 89

booming / flourishing / thriving 119

border 106

border formalities 106

border health check 104

border police / border force 107

botanical gardens 76

bottle (to) 54

bottle of wine 52

bottleneck / congestion / tailback / traffic-jam 95

bound (for) 92

box office / ticket booth / ticket office 74

brake (to) 95

branch lines 89

brandy / burnt wine 52

breakdown 96

breakers / surf 31

breeze 16, 31

bridge 78

bright interval / sunny spell / sunny period 17

bring back (to) 107

brochure / leaflet 117

browsing / window-shopping 76

buffet 45

burn / skin burn 109

bus / coach 74

bus lane 95

business 57

business class 82

business hours / opening times 76

bustling / lively 73

buy / purchase 101

by-pass / ring road / underpass 96

C

cab / taxi / taxicab 96

cabin 91

cable-car / gondola 14

cablecar / streetcar / tramway 79

call (to) (at) 88

call back (to) / return a call (to) 131

calm / peaceful / quiet / tranquil / serene 24

camp (to) / go camping (to) 31

camping 27

cancel (to) 80

cancel (to) (a flight) / discontinue (to) (an airlink) 86

cancellation / cancel (to) 25

capacity-building 70

cape 91

cape / point 31

capital / capital city 74

capitalize (to) (on) / cash in (to) (on) 122

capsize (to) 92

car accident 94

car licence 94

car park / parking-lot (US) 95

caravan / trailer (US) 94

cardholder / accountholder 102

careers in tourism / jobs in tourism 121

cargo-boat / freighter 92

carnival 74

car-park / garage facilities / parking facilities 25

car-pooling / car-sharing 95

carriage / car (US) / coach / railcar (US) 91

carrier / air carrier 87

carry (to) (passengers) 87

cascade / water falls / falls 8

cash 101

casino 31

castle 74

castle / chateau (pl. eaus / eaux) 27

cathedral 74

celebrated / famed / famous / renowned / well-known 49

cellar 52

cemetery / graveyard 75

chain of distribution 117

chains / snow-chains 8

chair (to) (a convention, a meeting, a session…) 60

chairlift 14

chairman 60

chalet 27

champagne 52

change 103

chapel 74

charter (to) (a plane) 80

cheap / inexpensive 102

check / search 106

check in (to) 26, 83

check in (to) / register (to) 26

check out (to) 26

check-in / registration 26

cheese 47

cheque / check 102

children's playground / children's adventure playground 25

church 75

cider 52

city / town 79

city car pound 95

city hall / town hall 76

city map 78

clamp a vehicle (to) / clamp a car (to) 96

clear the table (to) 46

clear up (to) 18

cliff 33

cliff / wall 11

climate 17

climatic 17

climb (to) / scale (to) 9

close off a letter (to) 127

closing salutations / closures 128

cloud 20

coast 32

coast guard 33

coastal development / shore development 30

coastal navigation 31

coastline / shoreline 33

coconut 32

code share / code sharing 84

coffee 45

coffee-shop / tea-room / tea shop 50

coins 103

cold weather / cold 18

collect frequent-flyer air miles (to) / earn miles (to) / gain air credit (to) 84

college / university 79

collision 88

come alongside (to) 91

comfort / comfortable 24

commission 102

commission (uncount / count) 117

commitment / involvement 65

commute (to) 89

commuter lines / suburban lines 89

company / corporation / entreprise 58

compare prices (to) 102

compartment 88

compensate (to) 100

competition 117

complain (to) (about) 100

complaint 129

comprehensive 118

compulsory / mandatory / obligatory 100

computer 121

computer hookup 61

D

E

F

fashionable / trendy / catching on 68

fast food 50

fax 128

fax machine 61

fax service 61

feasability study 119

feasibility study 66

feature (to) 49

fees 103

ferry / ferry-boat 92

festival 75

fever / temperature 111

film projector / movie projector (US) 61

finance (to) / fund (to) 119

financial year 119

financing / funding 66

fine / penalty 104

fine / ticket (US) 94

fingerprints / fingerscans 105

first flight 81

first-aid box / first-aid kit 114

first-aid hut / first-aid post 35

fish 49

fishing 69

fishing boat 31

fishing village 37

fitness 40

fitness centre 25

fitness programme 42

fitness room 42

fixed-price meal 47

flat / apartment (US) 27

flat swap / home exchange / house swap 28

fleet 83

flight 87

flight attendants 85

flood / flooding 19

flora 66

flow 119

flower show / horticultural exhibition 75

flu / influenza 111

fog 16

foghorn 36

folder 118

folklore 67

following… / further to… / with reference to… 130

food / fare / grub 48

food poisoning 111

footbridge 89

forecast (to) / foresee (to) / topredict (to) 122

foreign exchange / currency exchange 102

foreign exchange bureau currency exchange kiosk 102

foreigner (n) / foreign (adj) 105

forest 10

form 106, 128

foster (to) / promote (to) 70, 122

fountain 75

four-poster bed 25

fracture 111

franchising 83

fraud 106

freephone number / toll-free number 26

frequent flyer programme 85

fringed with / lined with 31

frost 18

fruit juices 48

fuel 81

fully booked / no vacancy / no vacancies 26

funicular / funicular railway 10

furnished 25

furniture (sg. a piece of furniture) 25

G

game reserve 70

gangway 93

garden 48

gas (US) / petrol 95

gastronomy 47

get a suntan (to) 31

get around (to) / get round (to) 75

get in touch with (to) / contact (to) 127

get lost (to) / lose one's way (to) 78

get off (to) (the train) 88

get under way (to) 91

gift certificates 24

give (someone) a lift (to) 95

glacial 10

glacier 10

glass-bottom boat 31

glazed frost / ground frost 18

globalisation 68

go camping (to) 27

go down a slope (to) / plummet down a slope (to) / ski down a slope (to) 8

go through customs (to) 107

go train-spotting (to) 89

gothic 76

gothic / medieval / romanesque / renaissance / contemporary style 78

grape harvest / grape-picking / grape-gathering 55

grateful 129

green areas / open spaces 75

grill / steak-house 48

groom (to) 8

gross domestic product (GDP) 122

gross national product (GNP) 122

ground (on the) 86

growth 118

growth sectors 124

guest house 28, 29

J

L

M

remain at someone's disposal (to) 128

renewal 108

rent (to) 95

repatriation 101

repeat (to) 132

repeat back (to) 132

report the loss of (to) / treport the theft of (to) 101

reputation 123

request 128

rescue (to) 13, 93, 101

research (uncount) 123

reservation centre 123

residence tax (US) / sejourn tax 27

respect 71

responsible 71

rest 42

rest area 94

restaurant / eatery / eating place 50

rheumatism 42

ride a train (to) / travel by train (to) 90

ridge 8

rise (to) / toincrease (to) 16

risks / hazards 101

river 13

road 96

road junction / crossroads 94

road network 96

road sign 95

road works 97

roadblock 94

roadstead 36

rock 13

rocky 36

roof 79

room rate 26

rope 8

round / round of drinks 55

roundabout 96

route 84

rucksack / backpack 13

rugged 32

rules / regulations 107

rum 54

run (to) / operate (to) 88

run on time (to) 88

S

safari 71

safe deposit box / private safe 25

safety / security 85

sail (to) 93

sailing 37

sailor 34

sample (to) / taste (to) / try (to) 48

sanctuary / henge monument 79

sand 36

sand yachting / land sailing / land yachting 31

sanitation 67

sauna / steamroom 42

savings 118

scarce 70

schedule 84

scheduled airlines (ant. non-scheduled airlines) 84

Schengen agreement 104

screen 61

scrub 40

scuba-diving 35

sea 34

sea air 30

seafaring 92

seafood 47

sea-front / ocean-front / waterfront 33

seagull 34

seal 34

seashells / shells 32

seasickness 112

seaside 31

seaside holiday / bucket-and-spade holiday (fam) 37

seaside resort / seaside town / coastal resort 37

season 21, 124

seat 85, 89

seat-belt 94

seaweed 30

second home 29

security bond / security deposit 27

sedative 113

seizure / confiscation 108

sell online (to) 125

seminar 60

serve (to) 50

serve wine (to) 54

service provider / service supplier 121

set menu / fixed price meal 48

shanty town 74

shark 36

shellfish 46

sheltered 30

sherry 56

shine (to) (sun) / twinkle (to) (stars) 16

shipping company 92

shipwreck 92

shopping arcade 76

shopping centre / shopping-mall (US) 74

shore / shoreline 36

shortage / lack (of) 69

shower 40

shrimps / prawns 32

shun (to) (a country, a destination) 117

shuttle 92

shuttle / shuttle bus 84

side-effects 110

sightseeing tour / tour 79

sign 77

sign (to) 130

T

U

V

Achevé d'imprimer par
Imprimerie Vasti-Dumas - 42100 Saint-Étienne
Dépôt légal : juillet 2008
N° d'imprimeur : 08-07-0140
Ref : 5054506/01
Imprimé en France